SLOPPY SECONDS:

THE TUCKER MAX LEFTOVERS

SLOPPY SECONDS:

THE TUCKER MAX LEFTOVERS

TUCKER MAX

BLUE HEELER BOOKS

815-A Brazos Street
Suite 220
Austin, TX 78701

Manufactured in the United States of America

10   9   8   7   6   5   4   3   2

Library of Congress Cataloging-in-Publication Data

ISBN 978-1-61961-002-6

CONTENTS

SPECIAL BONUS

INTRODUCTION

I started writing down my fratire stories in 2002, and ended up with three best-selling books, *I Hope They Serve Beer In Hell*, *Assholes Finish First* and *Hilarity Ensues*. I was pretty happy with that, and retired from writing any more stories at the end of *Hilarity Ensues*.

But after I finished *Hilarity Ensues*, I realized I still had about 50,000 words of stories that weren't published. So instead of just sitting on them and doing nothing, I did what any good author would do:

I put the remainders in a new book. This one.

But I didn't just stop there. If this is the first book by me you're picking up, and are unfamiliar with my three previous best sellers, that's fine, I've got something special for you:

I put my favorite story from each of my three previous best-selling books in this book.

So you not only get all my leftover stories, you get a free teaser from my first three books. Enough explanation. Go read, and I hope you have as much fun reading these stories as I had living them.

THE GOOD STUFF

FROM *I HOPE THEY SERVE BEER IN HELL:*

TUCKER TRIES BUTTSEX; HILARITY DOES NOT ENSUE

Occurred, Summer 1997

I spent the summer between my second and third years of college suckling on the parental teat in South Florida. It was the absolute prime of my "do anything to get laid" phase. Recently freed from a four-year long-distance relationship that began in high school, I wanted nothing more than to have sex with as many girls as possible.

Most of the things I did that summer are not story-worthy; you can only tell the same, "I got drunk on Dom and fucked this hottie" story so many times before it gets annoying. That summer I experienced every random sex situation that a 20-year-old can imagine: fucking on the beach, getting head from random girls in club bathrooms, sleeping with two or three different girls in a day, getting so drunk I passed out during sex, getting arrested for receiving fellatio in the pool at the Delano, blah, blah, blah . . . Jesus. What does it say about how fucked up my life is that I don't consider these stories to be extraordinary anymore?

Anyway, while most of my stories from that summer may not be extraordinary for me, there is one very notable exception . . . .

I was seeing one girl, "Jaime," about twice a week. She was a fresh arrival to South Beach, having moved there five months ago from Maine as a 19-year-old with a modeling contract. We met through a mutual friend who befriended her while they were modeling. Five weeks and lots of sex later, she thought we were dating. I knew better, but she was way too hot to bother correcting her assumption.

The ex-girlfriend of four years I previously spoke about was very sexually conservative. It was missionary in the dark and then straight to sleep, with maybe a blowjob on the weekends if she'd had a few glasses of wine with dinner (it was a high school relationship, I didn't know any better). After four years of this, I was ready to experience all the things I'd missed out on (when I wasn't cheating on her, of course).

Buttsex, known in the biz as "anal," was one of these unknowns, and I decided that I wanted to try it. Jaime was the perfect partner: very hot and very sweet but, more importantly, very naïve and very open to suggestion.

She was reluctant at first, not understanding why we just couldn't keep having normal sex, so I had to employ my persuasive powers:

Jaime "But . . . I've never done it."

Tucker "I've never done it either; it can be our thing."

Jaime "But . . . I don't know if I'll like it."

Tucker "You won't have to worry about getting pregnant."

Jaime "But . . . I like normal sex."

Tucker "Everyone's doing anal. It's the 'in' thing."

Jaime "But . . . I don't know . . . it seems weird."

Tucker "It's the preferred method in Europe. Especially with the runway models. Don't you want to do runways in Europe?"

After a few weeks of this, she finally consented. Though she agreed to let me put my penis in her small hole, she extracted a promise in return:

"OK, we can try anal sex, but I want it to be special and romantic. You have to take me out to a nice place, like The Forge or Tantra, NOT one of your father's restaurants, and it has to be a weekend night, NOT a Monday. And you have to keep taking me out on weekends. I'm tired of being your Monday night girl."

I made reservations for the next Friday at Tantra. Aside from being insanely expensive, Tantra is famous for having grass floors. Really; they put in new sod every week. They also advertise their food as "aphrodisiac cuisine." Yes, at that point in my life, I thought these things worked.

Thanks to my father's connections, I got us a corner booth in the grass room. She was quite impressed. I ordered like it was the Last Supper. No expense was spared. Two $110 bottles of Merlot, veal rack, stone crabs, the Tantra Love platter—it was lavish and decadent. I was 21, stupid, and wanted to fuck Jaime in the butt; I wasn't about to let a $400 tab get in my way.

By the time we left Tantra, this girl had doe eyes that would have made Bambi look like a heroin-chic CK model. She could not have been more in love with me. The entire drive back to my place she was rubbing my crotch, telling me how badly she wanted me to fuck her, how hot I made her, etc., etc. We get back to my place and our clothes are off before we even get in the door. We collapse on the bed and start fucking. Normal vaginal sex at first, just like always.

Now, what she did not know, and what I have not told you yet, was that I had a surprise waiting for her.

[Aside: Before I tell you what the surprise was, let me make this clear: As I stand right now, I am a bad person. At 21, I was possibly the worst person in existence. I had no regard for the feelings of others, I was narcissistic and self-absorbed to the point of psychotic delusion, and I saw other people only as a means to my happiness and not as humans worthy of respect and consideration. I have no excuse for what I did; it was wrong, and I regret it. Even though I normally revel in my outlandish behavior, sometimes even I cross the line, and this is one of those situations . . . but of course, I'm still going to write about it.]

This was going to be my first time foraging in the ass forest, and I wanted to have a reminder of my trip, a memento I could carry with me the rest of my life . . . so I decided to film us.

I planned this beforehand, but I was afraid she would decline, so instead of being mature and discussing this with Jaime, I just made the executive decision to get it on camera . . . without telling her.

That alone is pretty bad. But instead of just setting up a hidden camera . . . I got my friend to hide in my closet and film it.

No really—I know that I will burn in hell. At this point, I'm just hoping that my life can serve as a warning to others.

I left my door unlocked, and we arranged it so that around midnight my friend would go over to my place and wait until my car pulled in, and then run into the closet and get the camera ready. The top half of the closet door was a French shutter, so it was easy to move the slats and give him a decent camera shot through the closed door.

By the time Jaime and I got to the bed, I was so drunk I had forgotten that he was filming this, and of course she had no idea he was there. After a few minutes of standard sex, she kinda stopped and said, all serious and in her best seductive soap opera voice, "I'm ready."

I quickly flipped her over and grabbed the brand new bottle of Astroglide I had on my bedside table.

A week prior, after Jaime consented to buttsex, I realized that I didn't have any idea how to do it. How exactly do you fuck a girl in the ass? Luckily, I had the world's best anal sex informational resource at my disposal: The Gay Waiter. I consulted several gay waiters who worked at one of my father's restaurants about the mechanics of buttsex, and each one recommended Astroglide as the lubricant of choice. Much to my dismay, I learned that spitting on your dick is not enough lube for buttsex. Stupid, lying porn movies.

The other important piece of advice I remembered, "Make sure you use enough, because if this is her first time, she'll be especially tight, and it might hurt her. Use enough to really loosen her up and go slow until she gets used to it. Then it's smooth sailing from there."

Well, since some is good, more is better, right? At 21, this seemed logical.

I opened the cap, crammed the bottle top into her asshole, and squeezed. I probably emptied half of the four ounces of Astroglide into her. I have since learned from homosexuals that a four-ounce bottle usually lasts them about six months. So yeah—I overdid it.

But Tucker Max wasn't done. Oh no, after depositing enough grease in her to run a Formula One race car, I dumped half of what remained onto my cock and balls, really wanting to lube up because I didn't want her to be uncomfortable.

Really—consider my thought process: I was going to fuck her in the butt and film it without her consent, yet I was truly concerned about her personal comfort. Sometimes the contradictions in my personality amuse even me.

Predictably, I slid in with ease. She was a little tense at first, but with an Exxon Valdez-size load spilled into her poop chute, she quickly loosened up and got into it. I liked it also; it had a different feel to it. Not as good as vaginal sex, a little grainy, kinda tight, but still very nice.

Before I knew it I was fucking her like the apocalypse was imminent, burying it to the hilt with impunity. After a few minutes, I was ready to come. My urgency was expressed in my tempo, and I began really jack-hammering her. As the excitement got the best of me, I pulled out too far, and my dick came out of her ass. I kinda scrambled to grab my dick and put it back in so I could finish off inside of her, but before I could even get ahold of it and put it back in her ass, I heard a faint "psssst" sound and felt something wet and warm hit my crotch.

It was dark in the room (I was not smart or sober enough to leave the lights on for the camera), so after I looked down it took me a few seconds to realize that my dick, balls and groin area were covered in a viscous black liquid. I stopped moving and stared at my strangely colored crotch for a good five seconds, completely confused, until I realized what had happened:

"Did you . . . did you just . . . shit on my dick?"

I reached down to touch the liquid feces, still in complete and utter dis-belief that this girl shot explosive diarrhea on my penis, when, without warning, the smell hit me.

I have a very sensitive nose, and I have never been more repulsed by a smell in my life. The combination of synthetic Astroglide and the rancid stench of raw fecal matter came together to turn my stomach, which was full of seafood, veal and wine, completely over.

I tried to hold it back. I really did everything I could to stop myself, but there are certain physical reactions that are beyond conscious control. Before I knew what I was doing, it just came out:

"BBBBBBLLLLLLLLLLLLLAAAAAAAAAAAAAAAAHHHHHHHH"

I vomited all over her ass. Into her crack. Into her asshole. On her ass cheeks. On the small of her back. Everywhere.

She turned her head, said, "Tucker, what are you doing?" saw me vomiting on her, screamed, "Oh my God!" and immediately joined me:

"BBBBBBLLLLLLLLLLLLLAAAAAAAAAAAAAAAAHHHHHHHH"

Watching her throw up on my bed made me vomit even more. Her vomiting all over my bed, me vomiting on her ass, the next step was almost inevitable.

I heard the loud CRASH first, and turned to see my friend break through the shutters and rip the closet door off as he, the video camera, and the door tumbled out of the closet and crashed onto the floor next to us:

"BBBBBBLLLLLLLLLLLLLAAAAAAAAAAAAAAAAHHHHHHHH"

The memory of the two-second span where all three of us were vomiting at once is permanently seared into my brain. I have never heard anything like that symphony of sickness.

I think the crowning moment was when my eyes locked with Jaime's, and I saw her moment of realization and then her quick shift from shock and surprise to complete and irreparable anger. Between bouts of hurling she flipped out:

"OH MY GOD—BBBBBBLLLLLAAAAAHHHHH—YOU FILMED THIS, YOU ASSHOLE—BBBBBBLLLLLAAAAAAHHHHHH—HOW COULD

YOU—BBBBLLLLLAAAAAHHHHH—I THOUGHT YOU LOVED ME—BBBBLLLLLAAAAAHHHHH—OH MY GOD—BBBBLLLLLAAAAAHHHHH—I LET YOU FUCK ME IN THE ASS—BBBBLLLLLAAAAAHHHHH."

She tried to stand up, slipped on the huge puddle of backflow Astroglide on the bed, and fell into both my pile and her pile of vomit, covering her body and hair in vomit, shit and anal lubricant. She flailed on the bed for a second, grabbed the top sheet, wrapped it around herself, and started running out of my place. Still naked and retching, my dick covered in shit and lube, I followed her as far as my front door.

The last contact I ever had with her is the image I witnessed of her in a dead sprint, a shit, vomit and grease-stained sheet stuck to her body, running from my apartment.

Postscript

The camera we used was one of those ancient fragile ones that filmed onto a VHS tape, and when my friend crashed out of the closet, the tape recorder and tape broke. It didn't occur to us that the tape records the images magnetically, and we could take the actual tape itself and get someone to put it in another holster until after we had thrown it out. I know it seems stupid now, and believe me I kick myself about it every day, but you should have seen the apartment afterward—the tape was not a high priority. Astroglide, shit and vomit covered EVERYTHING.

I had to rent one of those steam cleaners, buy a new mattress, and I STILL lost my deposit. It was impossible to get the smell out. The next month was like living in a sewer. Every girl I brought back to my place after that refused to stay there, and some even refused to sleep with me anywhere because of how my place smelled.

What I never found out, and I still want to know, is how the girl got home. I never heard from her again, and the mutual friend who introduced us called her but didn't get her calls returned. I never heard anything about her or from her again, even though she left her clothes and ID at my place (she wore a tight dress out that night, and didn't bring a purse or any money with her).

Can you picture that scene? What did she do, hop in a taxi? Wave down a passing car? Get on the bus? She lived at least 30 miles away, there is no way she walked home. It perplexes me to this day. I'm hoping she reads this. Maybe then I'll find out how she got home.

TUCKER GOES TO CAMPOUT, OWNS DUKE NERDS

Occurred—September 2000

I went to law school at Duke, and as you may know, basketball is huge there. The demand for tickets, even for grad students, far outstrips the supply. In order to solve this problem, the people in charge make grad students camp out in a field to get into the lottery for the chance to get tickets. They expect you to spend a weekend sleeping in dirt and checking in every time they blow their whistles, like a fucking homeless kindergartener.

You think I'm exaggerating, don't you? This is taken directly from the Duke grad student website:

> "Welcome to Duke! Let's get right to the most important issue on your mind: How can **YOU** get season tickets to this year's men's basketball games in Cameron Indoor Stadium? Eligibility to purchase tickets is determined via the **Graduate and Professional Student Council Basketball Ticket Campout.** Campout for Duke Men's Basketball season will be held starting at 7:00pm on **Friday, September 8**, and runs through **Sunday, September 10**, at approximately 7am.
>
> The rules are simple: make it through the weekend without missing two attendance checks and your name is entered in a lottery. Lottery winners are then drawn and each of these lucky individuals is eligible to buy one of the 700 graduate and professional season tickets. . . .
>
> But Campout isn't just about basketball tickets. With almost 2000 students representing nearly every program and department at the University in attendance, this is also **the premier graduate and professional student social event of the year.** Campout is an excellent opportunity to bond with your students in your own program and make friends in other programs."

The bolding is theirs, not mine. Not only do they want grad students to spend their limited free time toiling in a parking lot, they are condescending about it. Either that, or they're just fucking retarded—do they really think that being stuck in a parking lot with 2,000 nerds is **"the premier graduate and professional student social event of the year"**? Not going to a bar or to a party with your friends, or, God fucking forbid, ACTU-ALLY GOING TO THE GAMES. Nope, to them, the coolest thing a grad student can do is to root around in filth.

I want tickets, so I have to go. OK, fine. But if those Duke basketball tools are going to make me sleep outside for two nights, I'm going to make them pay. And not just by getting drunk and fucking their ugly girlfriends.

It took me a few days, but I finally figured out how to completely ruin the event for everyone who sucks, while concurrently making it awesome for me and my friends. About two weeks before the grad student campout was to start, I was in the law library, intently focusing on my computer screen when my buddy Hate walked up.

Hate "What are you up to?"
Tucker "Ordering something online."
Hate "What, a Russian mail-order bride?"
Tucker "Better. A bullhorn."
Hate "What for?"
Tucker "For Campout. Look at this one, dude: It has a one-mile range! And a 110-decibel siren! It's made for police use!"
Hate [*ten-second blank stare*] "Jesus have mercy on our souls."

I paid extra for 2nd day delivery. When the day of arrival came, I was so excited I stayed home from class. Waiting for the delivery guy felt like Christmas, except without the part where your parents drink all the present money and wrap up things from your room as your gifts. Credit and Hate stayed home that day too, not because they were excited about the bullhorn, but because they are dicks. They wanted to taunt me until it arrived, knowing the anticipation was slowly killing me. (That, and none of us ever went to class anyway because law school is ridiculously easy.)

Credit "Max, I haven't seen you this excited since Brad Pitt took his shirt off in *Fight Club*."

Tucker "Credit, you're Jewish, your best friend is black, and your girl-friend is a cheating whore. Even if I *were* gay, I'd still have it better than you."

When the FedEx truck finally showed up, I sprinted to the front desk. I scribbled my signature, ran back to my room, tore open the package, loaded the batteries I already purchased, then cautiously put the bullhorn up to my lips and whispered:

"Hello."

My voice boomed out of the bullhorn so crisp and loud it shocked me. I felt a strange new power surge through me. It was like I drank from the Holy Grail. I took a deep breath and bellowed:

"WOOOOOOOOOOOOOOOOOOOOOOOOOOOOOOO!! CREDIT, I AM THE GREATEST MAN ALIVE!! HATE, I'M FUCKING INVINCIBLE!"

I ran out of my room into the living room. Hate was jolted forward in his recliner, white-knuckling the armrests with a look on his face like he'd just seen the devil. Credit had the same exasperated expression he got when he learned the student parking lot was a full mile away from the law school building.

Tucker "Holy shit! The volume's only at 6! It goes up to 10!"
Credit "Everyone is going to hate us."
Hate "Max, you aren't really taking that thing to Campout are you?"
Tucker [*into the bullhorn*] "We are friends and roommates, and yet . . . I feel like you don't know me at all."

I turned it down to 2—loud but still a manageable indoor volume—and spoke to everyone exclusively through the bullhorn for the next week. It became a part of me, a natural extension of my arm. I put it down only to shower and masturbate.

You know how when you pine after something really badly, like a cool toy or a new car or whatever, once you get it, it's never as good as you imagined it would be? This was the opposite. This was so much better than I could've ever dreamed. No possession of mine, before or since, has ever completed me the way that bullhorn did; it embodied all of the characteristics that I consider most essential to myself . . . and amplified them.

Arguing: I was pretty good at debating with people before, but now, I had a permanent trump card. How can you win an argument against someone who is louder than a chain saw? Even if you're completely right, you're wrong, because I have the bullhorn.

Humor: Everything you say becomes one level more humorous through a bullhorn. Stupid becomes passable, passable becomes funny, funny becomes hysterical, and hysterical becomes Dave Chappelle doing Rick James. I think this is because a bullhorn makes you so loud that it puts you on an imaginary stage. Just being the center of attention primes people to think you're funny—how else does Dane Cook get laughs?

Confidence: I was not lacking in confidence beforehand, but add a bullhorn and I became superhuman. It was like having a gun, except better. Walking around with a bullhorn gives all the authority of a gun, without any of the toolishness or danger of it accidentally discharging in your sweatpants. People just assume you're in charge and defer to you.

It was as if one internet purchase had suddenly made all things right in the world. Maybe the Duke nerds are right. Maybe this *will* be the premier social event of the year.

Campout started on Friday at 7pm, but me, SlingBlade, Credit, Hate, Jojo, and GoldenBoy got there about 5pm, so we could park our RV in a prime spot. As we pulled in and started to get situated—which for us entailed setting down the cooler and sitting around it drinking—I pondered my tactics:

Tucker "Alright fellas, what should my bullhorn strategy be?"

Hate "Break it. Or set it on fire. Anything that will get that fucking thing out of your hand."

GoldenBoy "Aren't you just gonna get drunk, yell at people, and not worry about consequences? Do you know any other way to act?"

Tucker "There is wisdom in your words."

At 7pm they blew the whistles for the first check-in. The Head Campout Nerd was giving instructions with one of those tiny little megaphones you can buy at Home Depot. He saw me and came over all excited, like we were friends:

Nerd "You have a bullhorn! I have one too!"

I immediately saw this encounter for what it was: my first chance to assert dominance over Campout. In the most condescending tone possible I said:

Tucker "Aren't you the cutest! And look at the toy Santa brought you for Christmas! You must have been a good boy this year!"

The dude visibly deflated. Here he was, hoping for a Bullhorn Buddy, and instead he got, well . . . me:

Tucker "What the fuck is that, a Speak & Spell or a See 'n Say? The frog says 'Ribbit'!"

He was about to say something, but I put my bullhorn right in his face and hit the siren trigger:

EEEEEERRRRRRNNNNNN

Tucker "Don't bring a knife to a gunfight, motherfucker. Take your Fisher-Price 'My First Megaphone' and

---

get the fuck out of my face. This thing is made for riot control! I run Campout now, bitch!"

The dude sulked off like the old lion that gets his ass handed to him by the younger lion and won't be seeing any more lion pussy. It was awesome. Only minutes into the start of Campout and I had savaged the only challenger to my authority!

Tucker "To be the man, you gotta beat the man! And now I'm the man! WOOOOOOOOOOOO!"
GoldenBoy "Rick Flair quotes? I know we're in North Carolina, but come on."
SlingBlade "Tucker is so proud of himself. He just bested a pimply, insecure 130-pound public policy student. Next up, *Romper Room Smackdown*."

The testosterone rush of my victory—on top of the beer I'd already drunk—put me into what could be called an "aggressive" state. Conversely, I was surrounded by the type of passive, fearful people who'd chosen to stay in school to avoid the conflict and consequences of real life. This meant I had in front of me a weekend where I could say or do anything I wanted, without worrying about anyone being able to talk over me. This must be what narcissist heaven is like.

Beer in one hand and bullhorn in the other, I began my symphony of awesome, starting off by verbally assaulting random passersby:

[*to a dude in a* Star Wars *T-shirt*] "Be honest, how many times have you jacked off to a picture of Princess Leia in her metal bikini?"

[*to a group of grad school students*] "You look like the type of people who would criticize a misspelling in a suicide note."

[*to this guy who had blond hair, was kinda fat, and wore thick glasses*] "If this were *Lord of the Flies*, you'd be dead already."

He foolishly turned to respond.

EEEEEERRRRRRRNNNNNN

Tucker "Silence! I've got the conch now, Piggy!"

[*to some random nerd*] "How hard was it choosing between the midnight showing of *Rocky Horror Picture Show* and Campout?"

[*to a chunky girl*] "Have you been tested for hoof-and-mouth disease!"

Chunkygirl "What?"

SlingBlade, who at this point was warming up to the idea of the bullhorn, took it from me and piled on:

SlingBlade "Tucker, you have it wrong. Clearly she has mad cow disease."

Chunkygirl "Fuck you!"

Tucker "You're right! She's frothing at the udder!"

Some European-looking dudes in Diadora shorts walked by.

Tucker "Fact: Soccer is a game invented by European ladies to pass the time while their husbands cooked dinner. Go practice your throw-ins, you cheese-eating surrender monkey!"

GoldenBoy "You just seamlessly stole a *King of the Hill* quote and a *Simpsons* quote to form one insult. I've never been this impressed by plagiarism."

Tucker "I'm awesome even when I steal."

Many beers later, I saw what looked like a hot girl far over on the other part of the parking lot.

Tucker "Man, look at her!"

Jojo and Credit looked over, and immediately started laughing at me. A lot.

Tucker "What? She's hot!"

As she walked closer, it became very evident she . . . was a he.

Tucker "Come on, he has waif legs and those tight skinny jeans and long hair—how was I supposed to know it was a douche Marxist and not a girl?"
Credit "He has a beard, Tucker."
Tucker "Does he? Shit, maybe I'm drunker than I thought I was."
Jojo "Yeah, that's it."

Everyone had a great time laughing at my expense. To this day, Jojo brings this up approximately once a month. It happened TEN FUCKING YEARS AGO. He's like a woman; he never forgets anything.

Tooling on idiots is fun, but I still have a penis, and it still demands its pounding of flesh, so we decided to see what good-looking—or at least willing—girls we could find at **"the premier graduate and professional student social event of the year."**

Dealing with grad school girls can be tricky. At Duke there were four distinct types: insecure, fearful types hiding from the real world; the super-serious ones so brainwashed by the unreality of academia they aren't even human anymore; the ones just looking for their Mrs. degree; and the sluts. Of all the types of women, I like sluts the best. Mainly because they are the most receptive to me putting my penis in their vagina.

A group of cute girls who looked like they might be game walked by.

Tucker "Ladies, you can't be the first, but you can be the next."

They looked at me suspiciously, as they should. Most of the time I don't know what's going to come out of my mouth, and sometimes, well . . . it's dumb. I've found the best thing to do when you stumble is to pretend that nothing happened and just drive forward.

Tucker "In addition to the bullhorn, we have beer! And we will share it with you!"

They laughed a little but didn't come over. I decided to go for the high-risk play. Nothing ventured, nothing gained.

Tucker "Look, here's the deal: If you're into immature, sexually compulsive men who drink too much and need to be the center of attention at all times, you are going to find me very attractive."
SlingBlade [*grabbing the bullhorn*] "Don't talk to this man. He has herpes simplex A, B and C. This was a public service announcement brought to you by SlingBlade."
Tucker "IT'S IN REMISSION, ASSHOLE!"

The fact that this exchange not only made them laugh out loud, but also got them to come hang out with us, should be all the info you need to know which grad school group they fell into.

But there was a bonus: They were in nursing school. We hit the slut jackpot! Slutty nurses not only want to fuck you, they want to take care of you too. They do you, then they do your laundry. This'll be better than Shark Week!

We talked for a while (without the bullhorn), when, just making conversation, I asked one girl about her favorite movie.

Girl "I love John Cusack, especially in my favorite movie, *Better Off Dead*."

Tucker "Oh no . . ."

SlingBlade "Did we ever establish why Lane Meyer couldn't be bothered to pay the paperboy? Why he tortured him for the entire movie, without any reason?"

Girl "That was funny. 'Gimme my two dollars!' I liked that."

SlingBlade "So you think that's cool, to take goods and services from people and not compensate them? Two dollars is a meal! That's two double cheeseburgers off the McDonald's dollar menu, which can be the only source of protein for those of us whose parents abandon all financial responsibility for their children at age 18."

Girl "Umm . . . calm down. It's just a movie."

SlingBlade "Whatever. You're clearly a selfish whore who would run over a puppy for a guy who shows the mildest interest. I'm sure you and Tucker will get along swimmingly."

The best part about hanging out with SlingBlade is he makes me look nice by comparison.

This girl wore a T-shirt that said FRONT LOADER on it. I couldn't figure out what it meant. She wouldn't tell me. This annoyed the fuck out of me, because I am smarter than she is.

Nurse "Well, if you're so smart, you should be able to figure it out."

Motherfucker. She leaves me no choice. Now I have to break her self-esteem, sleep with her, and steal the shirt.

I use a basic and well-worn tactic: I subtly disapprove of her for various reasons, so that she'll be forced to seek my validation. By sleeping with me. You know, the classy and mature way to get women. One particular exchange I remember:

Girl "I'm not a slut!"

Tucker "I mean, I want to believe you, you seem like a really nice girl, but . . . that's not what those guys over there said about you."

Girl "They did not! What guys?"

Tucker "I don't know, they left already."

Girl "They did not!"

Tucker "Well, let's try a little test. Now, you know everyone has their price, so how about this: Would you sleep with a guy for, let's say, 100 million dollars?"

Girl "Well, I mean, I don't know . . . yeah, probably . . . I guess."

Tucker "OK. Would you sleep with a guy for 10 million dollars?"

Girl "I don't know, maybe."

Tucker "OK. Would you sleep with a guy for 10 dollars?"

Girl "No, of course not."

Tucker "Why not?"

Girl "Are you kidding? I'm not doing that."

Tucker "We've already established that you'd sleep with a guy for money, now we're just haggling over the price."

I guess she doesn't have to learn history to be a nurse, because she thought my little Winston Churchill impression was funny and original. It went on like this for another several hours, me playfully disapproving, her seeking approval, until we snuck off to the back of my SUV and I gave her my full endorsement.

It was about 2am by the time we were done. After we finished, we both wanted to get back up and start drinking more. Plus, I think she was disappointed in my performance. That, or the fact I had been drinking, sweating, and blasting out meat farts all night made me smell like a Pakistani cabdriver. Whichever.

It had been pouring rain for over five hours, everything was soaked, and people were starting to go to bed. Which SlingBlade and I decided meant a prime opportunity to fuck with people.

But before I get into that, let me digress for a second to set the scene.

The most important thing you have to know about Campout is that it's not the same for everyone. There are two places to be: You can rent an RV or U-Haul, park it in the parking lot, and sleep in that, or you can pitch a tent in the field, which is at the bottom of a small hill. Even though the parking lot and field are only yards apart, they are very different worlds. RVs are nice; they have toilets, electricity, TVs, refrigeration, beds—all the comforts of modern life. Tents suck. They are nothing but walls made of thin fabric. You essentially sleep on the ground. Given the choice, most people would take the RV. But it takes money to rent an RV for a weekend, and the vast majority of grad students are broke.

Therefore, a divide develops naturally between the haves and the have-nots. The law students, business school students, and med students tend to be the ones with some excess money, so they rent the RVs and get to sleep in relative luxury in a nice clean parking lot. Pretty much every other grad school student—from political science to divinity school to environmental sciences—is stuck pitching a tent in the field below.

If it's a normal September weekend in North Carolina, this is not really that bad an arrangement. But this weekend it had been raining for days leading up to Campout, including that Friday. This meant the field the poor grad students were camping out in was completely soaked—quite literally a quagmire. It was like a huge mud-wrestling pit, except filled with loser nerds instead of bikini girls.

Which brings us back to the story: SlingBlade and I had, up until this point, spent all of Campout drinking and hanging out in the parking lot. We hadn't paid any attention to Tent City.

That was about to change. This was the moment I had been waiting for all week. I was Tucker Maximus: enslaved camper for an unwanted weekend, coerced supplicant for tickets that should rightfully be mine. And I would have my vengeance, in this life, right now.

Tucker **"Tent City! Behold, you live in filth! Your refugee camp for poor nerds is a cesspool of poverty and excrement! You are dirtier than the abandoned children of Bowery whores!"**

Some of the people who were out of their tents looked up at me quizzically.

Tucker "Tent City, do you realize how bad you smell? You are swimming in urine and feces. And for what? Crappy tickets to watch a shitty basketball team? You are a Christian Children's Fund commercial!"

One of them yelled out, "Shut up!"

Tucker "Tent City, query: Was it really worth it? Was it really worth the $30 you saved to spend the weekend mired in squalor and filth? [sniff sniff] I smell poop and bad decisions."

Someone yelled out from Tent City, "Shut up and go to bed!"

SlingBlade [*taking the bullhorn*] "Mom, is that you?!? STOP EMBARRASSING ME IN FRONT OF MY FRIENDS!!"

Four or five other law student friends came to join in. These weren't even my real friends, who were all asleep or being "mature." These were just guys who knew an awesome idea when they saw one, and they stood around drinking with us and laughing while SlingBlade and I continued to fuck with Tent City.

Tucker "Tent City, you are sleeping in mud and excrement. Don't believe me? I just pissed on this hill. Do you know what gravity is? Ask the physics grad students, they're down there with you because studying the underlying mysteries of the universe doesn't pay for shit!!"

Someone yelled out, "You know, there are things called BATHROOMS!"

Tucker "Toilets are for pussies and poor people!! I am a conquerer!"

Eventually some of the nerds had had enough and started congregating at the base of the hill. At its top, the hill is about 15 feet high and a good 15–30 yards from the people at the bottom. It was far enough away that you could see the people and interact with them, but not so close that you were near them in any physical sense.

RandomNerd "What gives you the right to keep us awake?"
Tucker "Because I have a bullhorn and you do not! Your fancy book learnin' should've taught you that the strong do what they want, and the weak endure what they must. Now bring me your finest meats and cheeses, and be quick about it!"

There were about six of them, and they all kept yammering at me. It was hilarious.

Tucker "I'm sorry, I can't hear you over the sound of how awesome I am. Please speak up."

They actually yelled louder.

Tucker "Again, I can't hear you, because . . . I HAVE A BULLHORN."

They kept jabbering at an even louder volume, and this one dude in particular was fuming. He kinda stepped forward wildly gesticulating at me.

Tucker "I want to keep doing this to see how long you will argue with a man who can speak 100 times louder than you. I bet you are sociology grad students; only an overdeveloped sense of justice can create this kind of indignation."

A few of them actually chuckled, and one girl nodded her head—I WAS RIGHT! Three of them, including the supermad dude, were soc grad students! And of course, this just made him madder.

There is nothing funnier than a disproportionate display of inappropriate and overwrought anger. You know, when someone really fucking loses their cool and completely explodes over something small? To me, that is the height of comedy, and I was determined to make this dude flip his shit.

Tucker "Oh, this is just awesome. Define 'post-structuralist' for me."

He actually started to define it! Like an idiot I laughed instead of letting him finish, and he immediately realized the joke was on him. Fortunately, all of us laughing at him must have taken him to his breaking point, because he walked a few steps up the hill and, shaking with anger, busted out this unforgettable quote:

SociologyNerd "'*Against stupidity, the gods themselves contend in vain!*' . . . Friedrich von Schiller!"
Tucker "HAHAHAHAHAH! Did you just quote a German philosopher at me? You're standing in mud and piss at 2am, and you just quoted a German philosopher at me?"
SlingBlade "I think he's calling you out."
Tucker "OK, I can play this game too. '*Stop ya cryin' heifer, I don't need all dat!*' . . . Mystikal!"
SociologyNerd "'*Wise men talk because they have something to say; fools, because they have to say something*' . . . Plato!"

I can quote rap lyrics until the sun comes up. But instead, I opted to come over the top and play the nerd trump card on him:

Tucker "Let's settle this once and for all. I'll give you the chance to save Tent City. Throw something at me—anything you want—and if you DON'T throw like a girl, I'll leave right now. I swear on my bullhorn."

The Sociology Nerd paused, thought about it, got a look of unbridled hatred on his face, adjusted his glasses, and stormed off in a huff.

SlingBlade "HAHAHAHAHHHAHA!!! IT'S LIKE LITTLE LEAGUE ALL OVER AGAIN!"

Tucker "You can run away to your burlap sack, but it won't save you from my bullhorn! I am the ruler of Tent City!"

All of the nerds got mad, but their anger never went beyond passive-aggressive complaining. People came and went, some people tried to yell over us, some tried pleading, some tried reasoning, and some just threw things (all like girls).

By about 3am, we'd woken up and pissed off enough people that something resembling a mob had assembled. But they STILL wouldn't do anything other than mill around and be angry. One tool in particular was fed up.

Tool "If we come up there, you're through!"

Unlike this bald-headed tool, I knew my Greek history, so I said the same thing to him that the Spartans said to Philip of Macedon when he sent them a message saying, "If I enter Laconia, I will level Sparta to the ground."

Tucker "If."

Tool "Yeah, IF, buddy, IF!"

It's frustrating when you make a smart joke, and even a nerd doesn't get it. OK, fine, let's see if he can detect condescension:

Tucker [*in baby voice*] "Who's dat widdle guy down dere making all dat big noise? He's jus so leetle! Coochie-coochie-cooo!"

That did it. Four of them got up their courage and ran up the hill. I know the one dude had just "threatened" me, but in the moment, it honestly didn't even occur to me that they would try to get physical. These grad students had taken our relentless mocking for hours because they were pussies. I mean, pussies *are* pussies—it's not just a word.

When they got to the top of the hill, they saw all my friends behind us that they couldn't see from down below, and they kinda stopped and milled around for a second, unsure of what to do. You know that scene in *Braveheart* where the two guys pretend to be lost so they can get the English to chase them, and the English take the bait, only to run into a huge group of Scots over the hill, and they become the prey? It was like that. Except with nerds.

Seeing their body language completely change, I figured this out . . . but was in such disbelief, I put the bullhorn down for a second:

Tucker "Wait . . . did you storm up here . . . thinking we'd run off?"

The embarrassed silence was all the confirmation I needed.

SlingBlade "HAHAHAHAHAHHAHAHHAHHAHHHAHAH! Oh my God, that's so precious!"

I fucking lit them up:

Tucker "WHAT ARE YOU GOING TO DO??? NOTHING!! YOU'RE GOING BACK DOWN TO YOUR MUDDY GHETTO! YOU CAN'T BEAT ME! I HAVE A BULLHORN, AND YOU HAVE NOTHING,

BECAUSE I AM SMART AND YOU ARE STUPID! NOW GET THE FUCK OFF MY HILL, YOU FUCK-ING PUSSIES!"

They milled around for a second more, then walked back down the hill. I don't know if I've ever felt more like a real warrior in my life.

Tucker "TENT CITY, YOUR PITIFUL ASSAULT HAS BEEN REPELLED! I AM YOUR CONQUERER AND YOU ARE ALL MY SUBJECTS! BOW BEFORE ME!!"

[*to SlingBlade*] "This is so awesome! This must be like what Alexander the Great or Genghis Khan felt like!"

SlingBlade "Jesus Christ, you are delusional."

Tucker "To be the man, you gotta beat the man! WOOOOOOOOO! And at Campout, I'M THE MAN! WOOOOOOOOO!"

I proclaimed sovereignty over Tent City for another ten minutes in various different ways, and after vowing to return the next day to continue my rule, we went to bed. After twelve hours of dedicated drinking, we'd finally hit our wall.

The Next Day

We didn't wake up until around 2pm. Once we beat back our hangovers with a 12 pack, SlingBlade came upon this one RV with an awesome spread of food—not just cheap hot dogs and sausages, they had gourmet shit. Judging by the quality and quantity, they were those rare type of grad students who actually had real money of their own, not just government loans. This can mean only one thing: business school tools.

In order to go to business school, you have to have worked for a few years and been good at it, so most of them have money saved. As a result, they not only have cooler stuff than the rest of us, they think they are better'n everyone. I decide to fix that for them.

I moseyed over, grabbed one of their bottles of wine, and started chugging it. A girl gasped out loud.

Tucker "Well, I'm sorry, your highness, but I happen to think wine tastes better out of a bottle!"

The entire group looked at me like I had just dropped a steamer in their shrimp platter, except one girl who laughed, so I talked to her.

FunGirl "So you're the bullhorn guys? I heard them planning your demise this morning in Tent City."
Tucker "I will crush their puny rebellion. Blood alone moves the wheels of history!"

As I housed their food and hit on the cute girl, SlingBlade tried to run interference before our inevitable eviction, but one bitchy girl was quite persistent:

BitchyGirl "Your friend brought a bullhorn to Campout? I mean, who does he think he is?"
SlingBlade "You must be lucky enough to not have met Tucker."
BitchyGirl "Why is he drinking our wine? And eating my pâté?"
SlingBlade "He has what the DSM IV refers to as Narcissistic Personality Disorder. Also, I believe that he is out of beer."

I think the fact that I was flirting with her friend actually pissed her off more than me drinking the wine and eating her goose liver. She was the type who would cockblock endangered pandas at the zoo.

BitchyGirl "Can I ask you a question?"
Tucker "If you wonder whether you're fat, you probably are."
BitchyGirl "Uhh . . . no, what I wanted to ask—"
Tucker "Yes, you could stand to lose a few pounds."
BitchyGirl "And you don't think you could stand to drink less?"
Tucker "Daddy drinks because otherwise he can't justify having sex with you."

BitchyGirl "Have sex with you? HA! You wish!"

Tucker "You can pretend you aren't into me to keep up appearances, but you know you're moist right now."

BitchyGirl "UGH! I could not find you more unattractive. You're slurring your speech, you have a shirt on that is two sizes too small, is covered in mustard stains and says FRONT LOADER on it, you reek of cheap beer and sex, and you clearly have a drinking problem."

Tucker "Drinking is a problem only if you're *not* good at it. To me, everything you listed is proof that I am *very* good at it."

BitchyGirl "You disgust me."

Tucker "I will not apologize for being awesome."

At some point we found ourselves at the Porta Potties. SlingBlade went into one, but I had to wait because the other was occupied. He came out laughing.

SlingBlade "I just dropped a deuce that could sink the Titanic."

Tucker [*I was so in shock, I put the bullhorn down*] "You took a dump in a Porta Potty? What is wrong with you?"

SlingBlade "Alcohol has made me impervious to your attempts at shaming."

The guy in my Porta Potty came out. As I opened the door to go in, I recoiled in terror.

Tucker "OHH! That is AWFUL!"

He started walking away, like everything was just fine and dandy.

Tucker "Hey you, come back here. Do you know what you just did in that bathroom?"

Guy "Yeah . . . I uh . . . sorry about that, man."

Tucker "Come here and smell this."

Guy "What?"

Tucker "DO IT NOW!"

Thus is the power and authority of the bullhorn: The guy actually walked back to the Porta Potty and took a sniff.

Guy "Yeah, so?"
Tucker [*angry astonishment*] "Yeah, so? That smell is not [*air quotes*] 'just went to the bathroom.' That is felonious assault on a toilet. You have raped my olfactory senses. Apologize."
Guy "What?"
Tucker "APOLOGIZE RIGHT NOW!"
Guy "OK, fine . . . whatever . . . I'm sorry."

Had we not been drinking for 24 hours straight, and had I not conquered an entire city the night before, I don't think I would have tried this. But the bullhorn had emboldened me:

Tucker "Now apologize to the toilet."
Guy "Dude, what?"
Tucker "Repeat after me: 'I am very sorry and greatly embarrassed that my excretory system could produce such a smell. I promise to eat more bran to prevent such things in the future.'"
Guy "Are you nuts?"
Tucker "I SAID DO IT!"

I was pretty much joking with the guy and fully expected him either to walk off or punch me in the face. There was no legitimate reason to obey me. I was just some drunk idiot yelling at him with a bullhorn . . . but he gave in and basically said it. After he left, I stood there in mild shock.

Tucker "Did I really just use the bullhorn to make a dude apologize . . . to a Porta Potty . . . for taking a smelly dump?"
SlingBlade "That thing is too powerful. It's like the One Ring that rules them all. After Campout, we have to find a volcano and throw it in."
Tucker "Let's make Hate do it. He hates the bullhorn, plus he's short like a Hobbit."
SlingBlade "Credit can go with him. He's a Jew, like Gollum."

———

We chilled the rest of the afternoon and evening, planning how we would fuck with Tent City again that night. But this time, the nerds had come prepared. They must have had spies watching us, because before we even got to the ridge to start our second assault on Tent City, they were standing there with a Duke cop. Still drunk on alcohol and the testosterone rush of the previous night, I decided to handle this the logical way, as I was Lord Tucker Max, Tent City Conqueror:

Tucker **"What's the problem, Officer?"**

DukeCop "You need to stop using the bullhorn."

Tucker **"What? Why?"**

DukeCop "The proper response to a lawful order is not 'Why?' "

Tucker "But Officer, I don't think you understand," [*I hold it in front of his face as if he hadn't seen it yet*] "I have a bullhorn."

You know that look a cop gives you when he's so confused that he doesn't even know how to respond? If you don't know that look, it means you haven't had enough fun in your life. He gave me that look.

DukeCop "You have to stop using the bullhorn for the rest of Campout."

Tucker "Officer, I can't stop. I am the ruler of Tent City!"

It was at this point the cop realized I wasn't crazy or stupid, just really drunk.

DukeCop "You're not in charge, you're not even on the Graduate Council. I am a law enforcement officer, and I am giving you a lawful command. You can obey it, or I can arrest you and confiscate the bullhorn."

I was not prepared for this gambit. I turned to SlingBlade:

Tucker "What do we do?"

SlingBlade "Stop using the bullhorn."

Tucker "Isn't there some way around this?"

SlingBlade "I don't know. I don't take Criminal Procedure until next semester. But I don't think so."

Tucker "Does it matter that he's a campus cop and not a real cop?"
SlingBlade "We're on Duke's campus. He also has a Taser. Taser beats bullhorn."
Tucker "Shit."

On Day 1, I subjugated all of Tent City. On Day 2, I was defeated by a single rent-a-cop.

To fuck with me, SlingBlade took the bullhorn from me and addressed Tent City:

SlingBlade "You are safe to go back to sleep. Tucker has been bested and the bullhorn problem is taken care of. I repeat, the bullhorn problem has been taken care of."
DukeCop "Hey! That means you too. NO ONE gets to use it again. If I have to come back, you're all getting arrested."

As I started to go back to my RV, head hung low in shame, I could faintly hear someone yell out from deep within Tent City:

"I guess the man got beat! WOOO!"

Motherfucker. Even ten years later, it still upsets me that my reign as conquerer lasted only a single night. I had so many people left to insult and piss off.

It's OK though, I got the last laugh. In the intervening years, my notoriety has made it so that all those people who were there, when they tell other people where they went to school, invariably have to answer this question, "You went to Duke? Did you know Tucker Max?"

I may have lost the battle, but I won the war.

Sexting with Tucker Max

Occurred, various 2009–2011

In the movie based on my first book, we wrote a scene where one of Tucker's friends tries to call him from jail after getting arrested. I thought it would be funny if the actor used my real phone number, so on set I had him replace the fake number with the "555" prefix you normally hear in movie phone numbers with my real phone number. In the real movie.

I guess it was funny . . . if you think thousands of random people calling and texting your phone every single fucking day for the rest of your life is funny. Who would've predicted so many people would call me if I put my real phone number in a movie? Well, pretty much everyone except me. It got so bad, I just said fuck it, gave in, and even secretly put it on the cover of my last book as well. Go look at the cover, you'll see it if you have half a brain.

[And yes, if you're one of the people who called, that really is my phone number, and no, I'm not going to return your call or come party with you and your friends, so you can stop leaving voicemails about that.]

Even though this outcome was totally predictable to everyone but me, one thing happened that no one anticipated:

Girls would sext me.

A LOT of them.

I don't know how many girls in America are into sexting, but I would guess that a large portion of them have tried to get me to respond to them at some point in the past two years. At first, all these girls annoyed the fuck out of me. Sexting is fucking stupid; it's only appropriate for re-pressed teenagers or attention-starved cockteases, not for grown adults who have *actual* sex with other adults. Look, either come over and actually fuck or stop bothering me.

Then it dawned on me: Instead of letting all these faux-whores annoy me, I should flip it on them and do what I always do when dealing with idiots: ruthlessly fuck with them.

I started responding to the sexters, and quickly realized I was in a unique position. These girls were already into me, so I didn't have to waste any time warming them up. They knew I was an asshole, so I didn't have to indulge any of their stupid bullshit, and yet they were STILL coming to me to sext? It was like the perfect storm of fucking-with-idiots comedy.

These are some of the funniest exchanges I had with these girls, divided into categories.

[Editing Note: For the sake of brevity and your sanity, I've edited these exchanges down to only the funny parts. No one wants to read the boring parts of sexting; that's like listening to fantasy football stories. I also removed some of the most obnoxious misspellings, emoticons and abbreviations, (e.g., fbgm, brb, <3, smh) to make everything more readable to educated adults who speak English.]

ABSURD

If I happen to respond to a girl's attempt at sexting with me, most of the time it's because I'm bored. In those cases more than any other, my responses are engineered solely to entertain myself. Her sexual gratification is so far down my list of priorities, that just typing those words out makes me laugh. At all times, my first, second, and third goal is to see how long I can get a girl to play along with the most ridiculous shit I can think up.

ABSURD #1: EVERYTHING IS BETTER WITH BACON

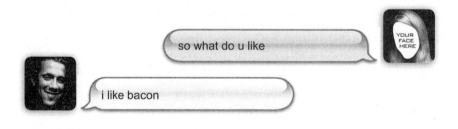

haha ok i like bacon too

i like how it feels when its rubbed on my skin

don't you think meat is sexy

i think ur meat is sexy

i have some fresh, lardy bacon

take the bacon and rub it on my penis

really?

then fellatio will be sexy AND sumptuous

how about i just swallow

i like how cum tastes

cum can't taste better than bacon

i dont really like bacon that much

YOU REVOLTING WHORE!

ABSURD #2: MARK OF THE BEAST

I push you down. Youre making too much noise

I kneel in front of you and start to lick your thighs

YOUR FACE HERE

I stand on the end of bed, naked, body glistening with sweat, grabbing my nuts in one hand and fist-pumping with other, screaming at the top of my lungs

lol

YOUR FACE HERE

RRRRRRRAAAAAAAAAARRRRR RRR!!!!!!!!!!!!!!!!!!!!!!

AAAAAAAAAAAAAAAAHHHHHHHHH HHHHHHHH!!!!!!!!!!!!!!!!!!!!!!

what r u doin?

YOUR FACE HERE

Sometimes a nigga just gotta hold his nuts and flex

uh,,,ok

YOUR FACE HERE

You clearly aren't into my masculine display. I go into the bathroom and don't come back.

no come back i like it

YOUR FACE HERE

You follow me in there. I'm pissing in your sink and pointing at myself in the mirror

lol thats kinda sexy

i walk up behind you and grab your muscular chest and press my tits against your back

I'm thirsty. Get me a beer

beer?

GET ME A BEER RIGHT NOW, OR I WILL POOP ON SOMETHING YOU CARE ABOUT!

ok ok I get you a beer

I have to drop a deuce. Youre out of toilet paper

No, i have some

I already used it all up. Get me some wheat bread.

not white, its unhealthy

bread?

ABSURD #3: RACIST FUCKER

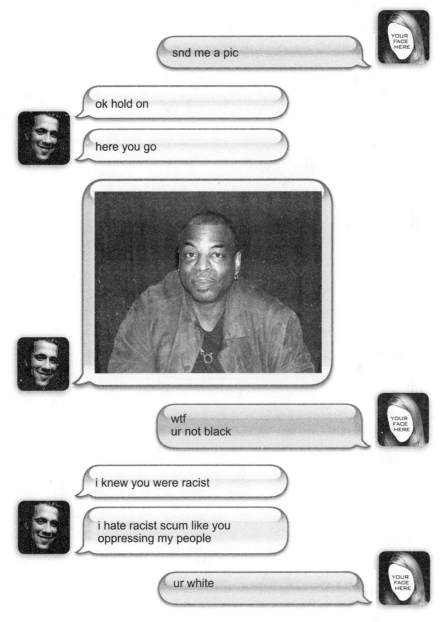

oh right LOL!!!!

there sure is egg on my face!!

here's a real one

what is that

They are rat balls

thats some animals balls?

Let me tell you about a rats balls! They are small, and they don't give a shit!

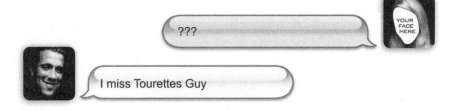

ABSURD #4: IMAGINE ALL THE POTTY MOUTH

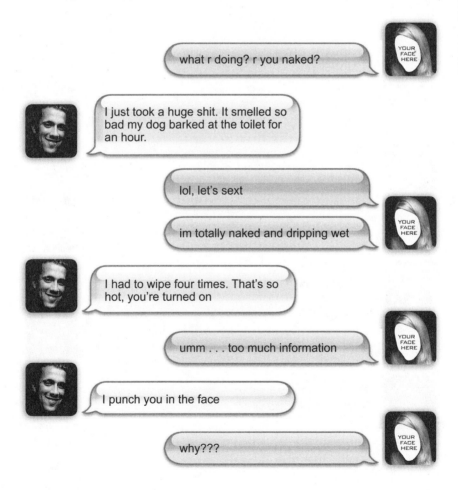

I won't tell you. You have enough information apparently

this is not sexting, this is stupid

This is how I sext. how do you?

You talk about the things you want to happen, like the things you are imagining with us

I imagine a world where there's no countries, it isn't hard to do

Sexual stuff!!

Nothing to kill or die for, And no religion too!

Wtf?

Imagine all the people, Living life in peace

Are you going to be serious?

I hope someday you'll join us, And the world will be as one

This is stupid be serious and sext

 Then we'll take a dump on Yoko Ono's bird chest

ABSURD #5: OMG I HAVE TO PEE

 Let's pray first

Pray?

Dear Lord, we give thanks for the sext we're about to have. We pray that you will watch over and protect us as we masturbate to the sexy words on our phone.

 And maybe you get your rocks off too if you want. Amen

rotfl

i'm praying you make me cum

 don't mock my god!!

he is vengeful!! you're going to get more wrath!

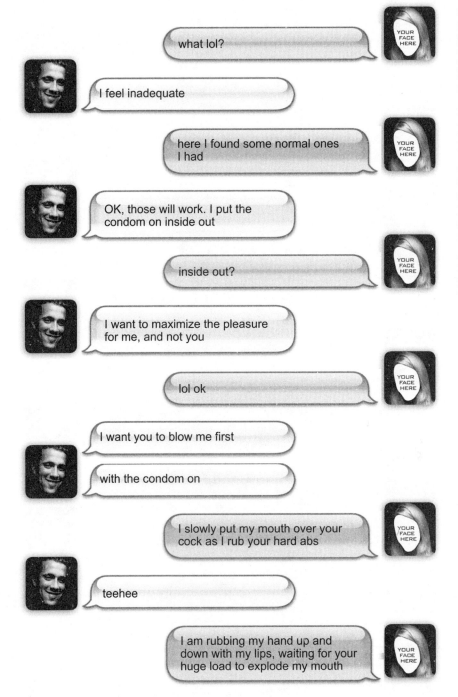

not sexy

 Sorry about your sofa, was it expensive?

Absurd #6: Metasext

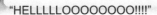

omg ur so good at licking my pussy

 Hello!

"HELLLLLOOOOOOOO!!!!"

Did you hear that echo?

your making my pussy dry

 Fine with me I can just put my dick in a garbage can and stir it around a little bit and it would essentially be the same thing

HEY!!! lol

 Be serious, I really want to sext with you

me too!

I gently push my tongue onto your clit, and vigorously flick it back and forth.

aaahhhhhhhhh

you are so good go harder

 I tease your pussy with my finger, ready to push it in and hit your g-spot.

ahhhh yea right there

faster i like it fast

 I stop and look into your eyes for full effect—ARE YOU TEXTING RIGHT NOW!??!?!?!

What? no!

I mean,,,what?

 So turned off. I can't believe youd do that i was trying so hard to eat your pussy good

i liked it what are you talking about?

 Worst.Sexter.Ever

Sexting with
Tucker Max: Mean

This may come as a shock to some of you, but I have a slightly volatile personality. I don't suffer fools well. And when I'm in a bad mood, I suffer stupid whores looking to sext even worse. It's not like I want to sext when I'm in a *good* mood. You really think it's going to be sunshine and kittens when I'm pissed off? The girls who persistently annoy me to sext with them find out.

Mean #1: Stupid Is as Stupid Types

tucker max, uv meet yur match!!

Not at spelling

haha looser

sorry I cant sext with you, I don't speak Stupid

im not stupdi!!

*stupid

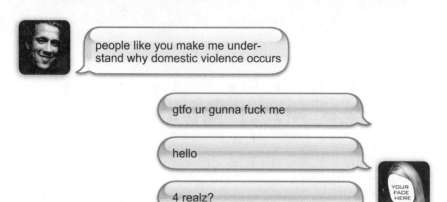

MEAN #2: THIS BLOWJOB BLOWS

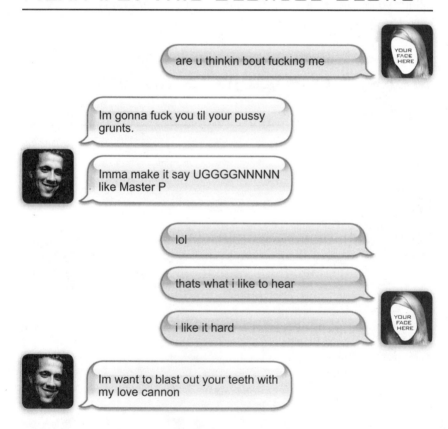

lol

I wanna go down on u first

 My penis is about to become a huge part of your mouth's life

I immediately take your whole cock in my mouth

My head goes up and down on your dick, flicking my tongue over it, savoring every inch

 Why can't you keep your teeth off my dick? I've never sucked dick, but it can't be that hard

Im giving you a perfect blowjob

no teeth perfect

 I've eaten popsicles before, and I managed to keep my teeth off those

im not using teeth

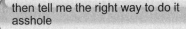 then tell me the right way to do it asshole

 This blowjob sucks. Where did you learn to give head? The Paris Hilton sex tape?

are you criticizing my sexting blowjobn??? this doesnt make sense!!!

 I'm going to have to talk to your family about this.

 my family?

 Your uncle told me you gave good head thats why I agreed to sext with you

 WHAT IS GOING ON???

 Look, your dog has his penis out

at least you turn someone on

THIS IS NOT APPROPRIATE

MEAN #3: HOOKT ON PHON-ICKS

lez sext

lol

I'd rather shit a knife

idk y u wnt sext w me

youre so dumb, I'd have to think of a different girl to finish

smh

wtf

SPELL OUT WORDS PROPERLY YOU FUCKING MOUTHBREATHER

y do u care abt grammer and capitalization

?

Capitalization is the difference between helping your Uncle Jack off a horse and helping your uncle jack off a horse

i dont get it

Wow. You're not even smart enough to realize how dumb you are.

lol

You've done something amazing. George Orwell would like a word with you whos that? some friend of urs? does he wanna sext or sumthin?

My head has exploded

 I don't know whether to masturbate or cry for the future

MEAN #4: WHORE ONSTAR

This girl was supposed to drive from her town about two hours away to fuck me here in Austin, and this exchange starts about the time she was supposed to be getting on the road. This didn't begin as sexting, but this dumb bitch drove me so nuts AND KEPT INSISTING that we sext, I lost it on her and tried to say the most offensive shit I could think of, to see if I could get her so upset she wouldn't even come over. It was impossible—like trying to rattle a 911 operator:

What ase you doing?

Happy Hour got to me and i wanna fCuk right now!

 How are you going to drive two hours drunk?

i'm trying to sobes up now So i can cum

not my fualt i like didn't eat anything today to look good for u what a moron. Don't come. You're clearly too immature to fuck me.

that's hard to do, but you did it

I'm not immature, I just didn't think a few drinks owuld do this to me. im sorry im gunna leave soon

on my way :)

you'll let me in right?

 You are a fucking moron. Or still drunk

Why are you being so mean?

Can I come now? Or are you like so mad at me?

 You might as well try. I can't think any less of you than I do right now. It has to get better for you

What does that mean? Lol.

Like 3o away. lol, you probably think I'm dumb don't you?

 Dumb seems smart compared to you

No I'm not! lol hahah i cna prove you wrong, but you'll think i'm dumb bc of my drawl lol

Maybe I can sing for you too! I sing country! lol!

i wont be talking much though, my mouth will be doing something else lol

 You've disgusted me so much I doubt I'll even get hard.

Well . . . idk. Take something. Or get drunk. lol.

Almost in Austin, whats the exact address?

 Jesus Christ. It's because of women like you that in no language on earth does the phrase 'smart as a woman' appear.

Just because I'm dumb don't mean I can't have sex you know lol. I look extra hot for you

 The hottest thing you could do right now would be to die in a firey wreck

lol your makin me laugh. I hope you don't mean that.

Take your steering wheel and yank it violently into the next concrete embankment you see. -That'll get me hard

What's an embankment?

You have to be kidding. Only dogs and retards are this stupid.

haha lol

Seriously whats the addy?

See that river? Aim your car for it.

quit lol! I called me grandparents and got the addy off the paper I left in my house. be there soon. are we just staying in for the night?

I do want you to do unforgiving things to me

OK, I'll throw you off my balconey

Lol thats a little too far, just up against the wall for me :) I love being fucked like that

im going to make you blow a homeless guy

lol no thanks only u :)

and you have to fuck a dog. And a camel. to prove your love

A camel? lol

I'm not a slut u know

can I stick a Mason jar up your ass?

hey I drink beer outta those! My asshole is tight, youll like fucking it.

Are you dead yet?

im about to be, textin and drivin.

turn your radio to full blast, that should complete the moron trifecta

Where is your place exactly, I can't find no numbers

i think im close

let's talk dirty more

I'm going to piss on you

Fine you can do that. But I'll squirt on your face while you eat me out. And you'll drown lol!

im gonna piss in your pussy

your gonne give me a huge load in my pussy

with your huge cock inside me

the only thing im putting in you is my maglite. right in your skull

lol stop!

fuck me Tucker i want to be tied up and you pin my legs behind your head and cum in my pussy

I want to bind your wrists so hard they turn gangrenous and fall off

I want you to flip me over and be the first guy to ever do anal with me

With a broom! That's so hot

lol nooo! I want to lick the sweat dripping down your balls

I'm going to give you a bunch of pain killers. Then drop you off at the homeless shelter

How many times have you woken up in a dumpster? Tomorrow will be +1

stop bashing me! lol

I bet your pussy smells like the dumpster behind an Olive Garden

 But your pussy has more food in it

That's a turn off . . .

 How much food DO you have in your pussy?

None??? sushi, lol. like in your book lol

start talking dirty, i just parked im so turned on

 I want to fuck you in a public park. Hard. So long and hard you pass out!

thats more like it ,thats so hot, i want you so deep inside me I can't even remember my name

And after you pass out, I'll leave you there, and let a bunch of dudes jack off on you, like a bukkake video. When you wake up, you'll have so much dry cum on you you'll think you've been baked into a pie

okay tucker, please stop, that is making me ill.

Fine, no gang rape, but when you wake up, you need to pick up all the dog shit people leave behind in the park. Some people are so inconsiderate of others.

Tucker! That's not sexting!!

And then I want you to eat it. Thats dirty, right?

You need to be civil with me.

That's not good sexting

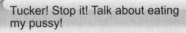

Tucker! Stop it! Talk about eating my pussy!

Porridge is just shitty oatmeal

What? lol

I parked on [redacted]. thats close right? Or should I park somewhere else

 Park in the least safe place you can find. Anywhere on Martin Luther King Blvd works

Where is that?

MEAN #5: POST "COITAL"

[this one picks up after I'd already told her I'd "cum" in sexting]

now i want you to do something amazing to me

whats the coolest sexual trick you know?

 My favorite trick is acting like the girl isn't there, and get my nut as fast as possible

I just did that trick

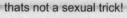

thats not a sexual trick!

 Oh . . . OK well, I know how to make the girl disappear after I fuck her. Thats a trick right?

no!!! thats not what I mean!!

i mean like licking my clit in a cool way

or fucking me some way where it like, involves a trick

u know, like, sex tricks !ol

Tucker?

hello?

Please don't interrupt me while I'm ignoring you

what?

your responding

no im not

yes you are!

u just responded!

what are you talking about, im ignoring you so youll leave

???????

whats going on

i dont want you to go

now I have to pay attention to my life again

MEAN #6: THAT'S (BEEF) CURTAINS

You reach down and rip my panties off. You want my pussy so bad you are rock hard

I tease you and make you stare at it for a minute

 I'm confused. It kinda looks like a cheeseburger turned sideways.

a cheeseburger?

lol. be serious! Now you go down on me

 OK, I'll eat you out. I move slowly down to your pussy

im so hot now, I want to just push your face right into my pussy, but ur too strong

I'm having trouble here. I can't really eat you out with this gas mask on

What? Gas mask?

I don't know what's been in your pussy

!ol quit!

Have you been tested?

YES!

You are turned on and want to eat me out!

OK, I'm so turned on, I take the gas mask off, say a prayer, and lick your pussy

Oh yeah, lick it hard, bite me on the clit

I'm having trouble again

?

I spread open your labia in search of the clit. It looks like I am opening a burnt grilled cheese sandwich.

71

omg im gonna puke

ur ruining it

you're ruining it! Puking is for AFTER sex!

FUCK OFF UR FUCKING DISGUSTING

whatever, im hungry anyway

When I put my face on your pussy, it plugs my nose and I can't breathe properly.

just lick my clit like you said

OK, but your pussy is so fat, I can't really find your clit

I DO NOT HAVE A FAT PUSSY!

MEAN #7: NAIL IN THE COFFIN

You slowly drag your tongue down my thigh

Hey, there's a sign on your crotch!

MEAN #8: ABORTION > DEAD BABY JOKES

I rub your belly and softly whisper in your ear . . . "Im gunna put a baby in there"

Noooo

 why not? well make beautiful abortions together . . .

don't joke about that

ok no jokes about babies.

except this one

 you know whats harder than nailing a dead baby to a tree? nailing it to a dead puppy

stop seriously dead baby jokes r not funny

 have you ever tried to nail a dead baby to a dead puppy? its hard!

omg im gunna vom

seriously stop dead baby jokes they r awful

 no they are awesome

not to me I had an abortion

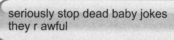

Hold on—its not ok for me to make a dead baby JOKE, but its ok for you to make an ACTUAL DEAD BABY????

FUCK OFF AND DIE!!

is that what you said to your baby after the abortion?

hello?

mommy are you there? it's me, your dead baby

why didnt you love me?

Sexting with Tucker Max: A/S/Location, Location, Location

Some of the girls who sexted me were into pretending we were in weird, exotic locations, except they always left it to ME to pick the place. Like because I'd written a book about fucking lots of women, all of the sudden I was some kind of connoisseur of imaginary exhibitionism. I didn't understand this at first—not only do you want to have fake sex, but you want to do it in a fake place NOT of your choosing??—and I eventually learned to stop trying. Fools act foolish; that's what they do. You can't actually try to understand them; you just have to go with it.

So I did, and they turned out to be some of the funnier exchanges.

Location, Location, Location #1: Pussy Pussy

let's fuck at the zoo!

the zoo? thats weird

YOUR FACE HERE

well, I like it when animals watch me fuck

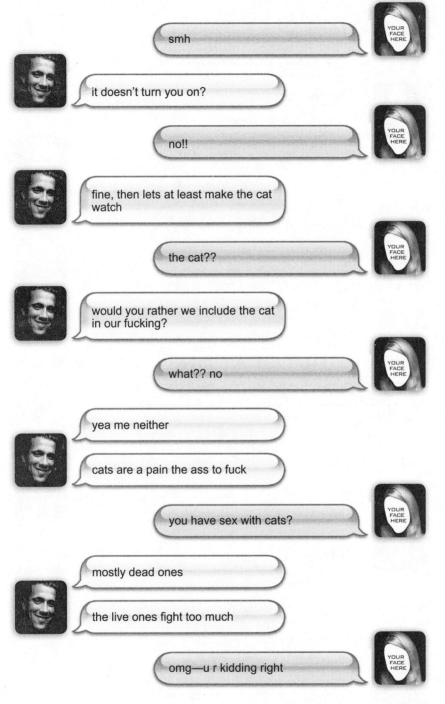

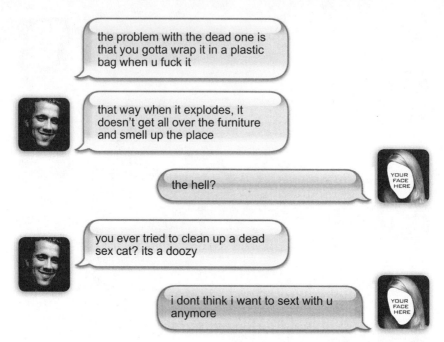

the problem with the dead one is that you gotta wrap it in a plastic bag when u fuck it

that way when it explodes, it doesn't get all over the furniture and smell up the place

the hell?

you ever tried to clean up a dead sex cat? its a doozy

i dont think i want to sext with u anymore

LOCATION, LOCATION, LOCATION #2: PLAYOFF READY

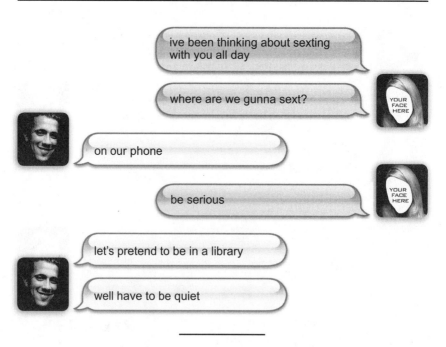

ive been thinking about sexting with you all day

where are we gunna sext?

on our phone

be serious

let's pretend to be in a library

well have to be quiet

lol thats hot

i want you in the stacks like in college

this is a public library

its mostly just crappy dvds and sleeping bums

ugh ok

i want you on some books

ok i have to poop first

you find the sexiest book for us to fuck on

lol how about your book

i have masturbated to it before

Im in the bathroom stall

ow. the poop is hurting

now its feeling good

haha ok

there's some kid outside the stall yelling about needing to dookie

HEY SHUT UP KID!! IM SHITTING IN HERE!!

loi dont be mean!!

my shit smells

I can hear the kid dry heaving from the smell

gross

I hogged the stall for so long, the kid shit his pants and ran crying to his mother

I WIN!!

r u done pooping? I want anal in the library

lol

I just took a shit so big that I'm having postpartum depression

r u into s&m & stuff? lets do that

LOCATION, LOCATION, LOCATION
#3: 8 MILE

where r we fucking?

idk

let's sneak into a trailer park and fuck in some bumpkins double wide

ahaha rotflmao!!!

ok lets do it

so we're in the trailer park. its shitty lots of broken down cars

trash everywhere

lol is there such thing as a nice trailer park?

let's go into this trailer, the concrete blocks that its on are not rotted

it should support our fucking

lol ur crazy

I grab you by the hair and kiss you

i kiss you back

i rub ur cock thru ur pants its so hard and big

these curtains are really crappy. who designed this place? They should be ashamed of themselves

i pull ur hard cock out and stare at it

i cant stand these floral patterns anymore, so i push you to the bedroom

i lay on the bed and cant wait to get my pants off

UGH! It's the same patterns in here? When did they buy this stuff, 1970?

just cum fuck me!

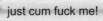

I grab my cock and dive right into your pussy!

hey—why are children running around in here?

?? idk

they got dirty faces and no shoes

they keep yelling about lunch

what r u talking about?

These aren't your kids?

what kids!! were fucking on the bed

I know, but these damn kids are distracting me!

they keep yelling about wanting push pops and cans of frosting for lunch

r we gonna sext or not?

they think you're their mom

are you?

no!

since im humping their mom, i think its only fair they get some candy for lunch

give them money or whatevs

this is stupid lets sext

dont you realize the children are our future?

dont you care about your kids?

THEY ARE NOT MY KIDS!!

seriously though—who eats frosting straight out of the can?

let's grab one of these kids and give it a good shaking

how is this sexy to you?

shaking children is pretty much the tops

LOCATION, LOCATION, LOCATION
#4: THE CLAMBURGLER

lets sext

Where are we sexting?

I grab your hand and we walk inside. Hey look, there are new items on the dollar menu!

 who cares were here to fuck

 Look at the a retard mopping. Don't you think it's nice that McDonalds hires the mentally handicapped?

lol

 i pull you into the first booth and slide my hand down your pants you are so hard

 Don't you think people will see us here?

WHATEVER we find a booth that is secluded

 you put your hand on my breast and kiss me deeply

 I kiss you back and grab your tits hard

Wait, but should we eat first? I'm kinda hungry

 no lets fuck im so horny

But if I don't eat Ill have low blood sugar, and I really want to fuck you the best I can

ok fine. but youd better fuck me so hard I can't walk tomorrow

You sound like Emily Dickinson

who?

Just some whore I banged who writes all this poetry about me. LAME

What do you want to eat?

lol

maybe get something we can use with sex, like chocolate syrup

I don't like mixing semen and food

i dont care, just get a big mac whatev

I can't eat a big mac. I eat paleo, no grains

jsut get something!! lol

I start to order, but I get distracted. There is a ginger working the register

 ginger? like a redhead?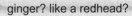

 Yes. And he has cornrows. This makes me VERY uncomfortable

lol thats weird

 A fat woman comes in. She's so big she has to ride one of those motorized scooters

I say in a deep, mysterious voice, "We've been expecting you."

omg lol that would be halarious

 I decide to ask her something Ive always wondered about

-"How do you wipe? I mean, you are clearly too fat to reach your own asshole. Do you tie a rag on a stick?"

OMG LMFAO

She starts crying and slowly rolls her scooter out

as the handicapped doors open, she lets out a sloppy wet fart

it sounds like someone burping with a mouth full of pudding

lol ur so funny lol

Now Im really turned on

I grab you and pull you into our secret hidden McDonalds booth

I pull your penis out of your pants its so hard i cant resist and start sucking it right away

thats right, suck it good, suck it like its a mcflurry bitch

I massage ur balls and groan as I deep throat you

I am getting wet u reach down and start massaging my clit

Your pussy is so wet, it sounds like theres water splashing everywhere

im so wet ur fingers are all in my pussy

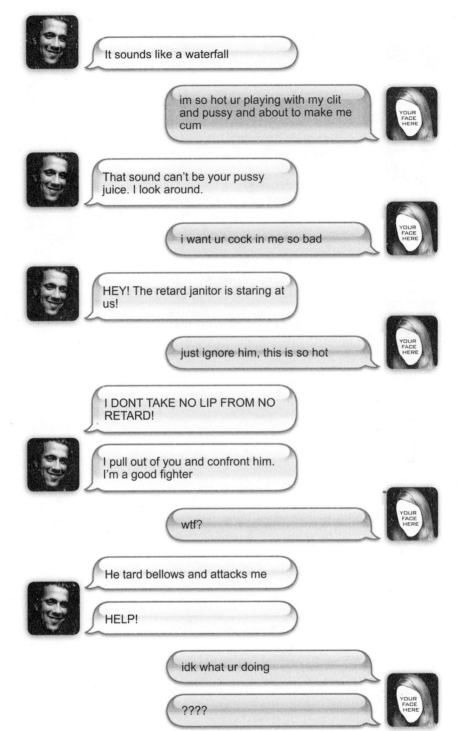

Too late. He's too strong. He whipped me with his retard strength

lol?

I don't think I can finish now, he really hurt me.

this is the weirdest sexting ever lol

Now he's asking me for candy

Do you have any Jolly Ranchers in your purse?

THE LEFTOVERS

TUCKER GOES TO MUSLIM WEDDING, DRINKS ANYWAY

Occurred, August 2002

One of my best friends from college was a tiny little Muslim girl, Famina. We couldn't have been more opposite—she was sweet, compassionate, caring, conscientious, while I was, well, me. But despite these differences, we were super close all through college (and no, we never hooked up, and yes, it's possible to have platonic friendships—especially when the girl refuses to hook up with you).

So when her wedding came along, of course she invited me, even though it was going to be a traditional Muslim wedding full of traditional Muslim people. That means six hours of no alcohol, no single girls who will have sex with me, and nothing but Indian food. Oh happy joy!!

To make matters worse, the girl who I was supposed to bring as a date canceled on me five hours before the ceremony. Why? I don't know. That's the problem with being a narcissist: Things you do that don't even register to you can sometimes be huge insults to other people. I mean, how was I supposed to know she didn't want to know that dress really did make her look fat? Oh well, if she can't take a joke, fuck her.

Wedding starts at 6pm. I crack my first beer at 2pm and call Famina's maid of honor, Samira, who is also a good friend of mine from college. I don't say hi when she answers, I just let out a loud obnoxious belch.

Tucker "BBUUUUUUUUURRRRRRRRRRRPPPPPPPPP!!"
Samira "Tucker! Have you been drinking?! Before Famina's wedding?!?"

Tucker "Hey, these beers aren't going to throw themselves up."

Samira "TUCKER!"

Tucker "You guys were kidding about there being no liquor at the wedding, right?"

Samira "No, silly! It's a Muslim wedding!"

Tucker "Well, is it B.Y.O.B.?"

Samira "NO! It's B.Y.O—NOTHING!!"

Tucker "What? That's kooky talk. How am I supposed to go to a wedding without drinking?"

Samira "You can't drink! Almost everyone there will be devout Muslims."

Tucker "So you get to fly planes into our buildings, but we can't drink at your weddings?"

Samira "Tucker! We're Indian, not Arab! You know this!"

Tucker "If it's brown, shoot it down."

Samira "Tucker!"

I figured that settled the issue. Famina and Samira have known me for eight years, since I was a freshman in college and I would stay up late with them during Ramadan, eating awful Indian food they would cook on hot plates. They know what I'm like.

I run through all the beer in my apartment and start on vodka and club soda. By 5:30, I'm pretty blitzed. I don't own any nice clothes, so I have to "borrow" my roommate's black Armani suit to wear to the wedding. And because I don't even own a button-down shirt, or a tie, I put on a white t-shirt underneath. I put the flask of Popov vodka in one back pocket and flask of Montezuma tequila in the other. I looked like I should be running numbers for a Russian crime syndicate.

I arrive at the reception hall, and I am literally one of about 14 white people. Everyone else—all 250 plus—are Indian. And these aren't casino Indians. That'd be great—then you'd know there would be liquor there. Native Americans take their firewater seriously. No, these are dot Indians. Mostly Gujarati, but from what I can tell, there are also Hindus, Haris, and Bengalese. And all of them are either Hindu or Muslim.

I immediately go to the bar. It has a wide selection of water, juice, and soda. The bartender looked like the type who was probably the star of his high school play. I ask him for two glasses of ice, one with a little Sprite, the other with a little Coke, "Not filled to the top." He gives me one of those judgmental sneers that only gay guys can do right. Fuck him.

I carry my drinks to the bathroom, where I have to ask some dude in a full-on, Afghanistan-style beard for assistance in opening the stall door, because you know, my hands are full. Govinda eyes me suspiciously. Fuck him.

I down my first couple of makeshift highballs, trying to avoid the dull reflection in the toilet seat dispenser. God forbid I'm forced to consider that perhaps my life is in shambles if I am sneaking liquor into a Muslim wedding and drinking it on a toilet seat. I drench this thought with vodka and tequila and drive on.

Wandering around trying to find someone to talk to, I realize that I know very few people at this wedding. All of the people I know are either relatives of Famina, and thus hate me, or are from the University of Chicago, and thus hate me. So I find the people who either work with or went to college with the groom, Barry.

Within 15 minutes, they hate me. Why? If you know anything about Indians, they are all about status; in fact, pretty much universally the first question they ask you is, "What you do for a living?" Well, I had just started writing at the time, and I didn't really have a job, so I decided to fuck with them:

Girl "I'm a dancer."
Tucker "Really? Pole or ballet?"
Girl "What?"
Tucker "Nothing."
Girl "So, what do you do?"

Tucker "I'm not really sure."

Girl "You're not sure? What is your job then?"

Tucker "Well, I guess I'm a writer."

Girl "A writer? Would I have read anything you've written?"

Tucker "If you'd read something of mine, you wouldn't be talking to me right now."

Girl "Well, what have you published?"

Tucker "Umm . . . I wrote a children's book."

Girl "Really? What's the title?"

Tucker "It's called *The Boy Who Died From Eating All His Vegetables.*"

Girl "What??"

I convinced this one girl that I lived in Cabrini Green (a legendarily awful, crime-infested housing project in Chicago), and invited her to come visit me.

Her "If I go, won't I get shot at and murdered?"

Tucker "No, that's ridiculous, of course you won't get murdered. Pretty girls like you get raped."

She didn't find this very funny. So I started talking to this very old Indian woman who looked like she was made out of juiced grapes, and turned out to be the previous girl's mother:

Woman "What do you do?"

Tucker "I'm a fluffer. You know, for porn movies."

Woman "What is a fluffer?"

Tucker "Ask your daughter, I bet she'll know."

To a bridesmaid:

Bridesmaid "So what do you do?"

Tucker "I'm a freelance pet euthanizer for local animal shelters."

I thought she was going to cry.

Tucker "Don't get upset; I do it quickly. I only make the ugly dogs and cats suffer. I kill the cute ones quickly. It all depends how high you hold the bowling ball before you drop it on their skull."

I didn't see her at all after that.

After the "cocktail" reception, we all filed into the auditorium for food and speeches. They were pretty much across-the-board terrible, but one stood out: the best man's speech. It was like watching Stephen Hawking try to swim. The dude tried to be funny, but his idea of comedy was so awful he might as well have just asked us to watch a stillbirth. Actually, that would have been funnier.

Then we ate. The English LOVE Indian food—that should tell you all you need to know about Indian food. It sucks. But this was okay for sucky food, I guess. Most of it was vegetarian though, which confused me. I kept asking everyone, "If we aren't supposed to eat animals, then why are they made of meat?" No one had a good answer.

After dinner, Famina's dad put on a slide show. I think it was her dad; I don't really know. Everything got blurry right around that point, which coincidentally was right about the time I finished off both pints I brought with me. Perhaps tellingly, I didn't even think I was that drunk. I didn't feel drunk. But who really ever knows how drunk they are, right?

Well, everyone at my table knew, because I passed out in my seat during his slide show.

NANTUCKET SUCKS

Occurred, July 2005

I have a lot of great stories that revolve around drinking, sex, and partying. This is not one of them.

I was going to Nantucket for a weekend. My buddy Chevy was staying at his parents' house there with some friends, and swore to me I'd have a great time if I came out.

I was in LA for the summer for work, so I had a long flight ahead of me. I figured I'd just read and nap. I took my seat and it became immediately evident that napping wasn't going to happen. I had a middle seat. In coach. In the window seat was a guy who looked and smelled like he was about to ask me for some spare change. In the aisle seat was an obnoxious slob, spilling grease all over his shirt as he stuffed nasty Sbarro pizza in his face and yelled at his dopey, ill-disciplined children across the aisle.

I decided that I was not going to sit in coach. I decided that I was better than these and deserved better accommodations. I'm moving to first class.

Once I decided I was going to sit in first class, I ran into a series of problems:

1. I didn't have an upgrade voucher.
2. I didn't know anyone who worked for this airline.
3. I was not a member of any sort of Elite Gold Ultra Club.
4. I didn't have $1500 to pay for an upgrade.

Which pretty much derailed the plan.

Most people would stop here. But I'm not most people, I'm Tucker Max, and I'm going to find a way around this.

I thought and thought, running through all sorts of ridiculous permutations of plans. Then it hit me. The most obvious solution in the world, I cannot believe I've never thought of it before. I waited until most of the plane filled up, and saw that there were still three empty seats in first class, so I summoned the my A-game charm, and approached a young female flight attendant in the back cabin:

Tucker "Hey, how are you?"
FA "Hi, good."
Tucker "I really hate to bother you about this, but can you possibly help me out?"
FA "Yeah, what can I do for you?"
Tucker "Well, when my people booked my flight, they made a mistake and put me in coach. I hate to make an issue about this, but is there any way you can move me to first class? Normally I would just live with it, but I've already had a few people pestering me for autographs and it's a long flight . . . and I just can't get any work done back here with everyone trying to get a piece of me. I'm sure you know how it is. I can't be the first person you've had this happen to."
FA "Oh my gosh, yeah, no problem. Hold on, let me just make sure we have room, I'll upgrade you right away. Stay right here."

Remember, this was 2005, before my first book even came out. NO ONE knew who I was, I was completely bullshitting her. But it worked. Three minutes later, I was in first class throwing back free beer and putting complimentary slippers on my feet. No one "bothered" me the rest of the flight, and none of the flight attendants even asked who I "was."

After a few beers, I noticed the guy sitting next to me. He was a few years older than me, mid-thirties, clean cut, wearing normal clothes—but he had a huge bulge on his hip. Well, he wasn't black, so it couldn't be his dick . . . this motherfucker was packing a gun.

Tucker "I hope to God you're an Air Marshal."
Guy "I'm not an Air Marshal."
Tucker "Great, Al Qaeda then?"
Guy [laughs] "Don't worry, I'm FBI. I'm off duty, but we're required to carry our sidearms whenever we fly."

We got to talking and trading stories. I told him "The Buttsex Story," which he thought was hilarious, so in exchange, he told me an FBI story:

"At the FBI Academy, there is this simulation where you shoot at a huge screen. They throw scenarios at you to teach you how to react to them. Kinda like a video game, but life size. You even get a pneumatic gun that feels just like a regular gun when you shoot it, with a recoil and every-thing, but it only shoots a laser, obviously.

Well, in one of the scenarios you are in a hallway trying to clear a house and a 12-year-old kid comes around the corner with a gun at his side. He walks around in a daze, and you are supposed to react to what he does.

When I did the scenario, as soon as he came around the corner I told him to drop the gun, he didn't, so I started lighting him up. But strangely, he wouldn't go down. It was so frustrating; I knew I was hitting him, because the little red dots were hitting him center mass, but he wouldn't go down. I emptied the first clip, slapped another one, and kept firing.

By the time he went down, I had advanced right up onto the screen, and was about to start pistol-whipping the canvas. I couldn't figure out what was going on. He finally dropped on the 17th and 18th shots. I added the 19th when he was down, just for good measure. I wasn't taking chances with the Bionic Twelve-Year-Old.

The lights come on and the instructor was in total shock, 'Do you know why you had to shoot 19 rounds? The simulation ISN'T EVEN SET UP

TO REGISTER SHOTS THAT EARLY. I've NEVER seen anyone RE-LOAD in that scenario before!'

Apparently, since the weapon was only at his side and not raised, we were supposed to yell some jibberish about 'This is the FBI,' and something else along the lines of, 'Put down the weapon,' and then give him time to comply before we fired. I wasn't having it. You don't brandish a weapon at Agent Jones and live to tell about it.

I got into a 30-minute argument with the instructor about how to write it up cleanly. I won, and he passed me."

What a cool dude. This was a plane seating jackpot, but . . . I had to call him out on something:

Tucker "You can't just plug kids like that. Dude, I went to law school and I know there is no way a cop could do that and get away with it."
Agent Jones "Oh no, of course not. Cops are different. They have very different force continuum rules than we do."
Tucker "Force continuum?"
Agent Jones "Basically, it means when you are allowed to initiate force on a criminal. Cops have a whole ordeal they have to go through, warning the criminal, giving him time to stop, etc. For the FBI, it's not like that. If there is an immediate threat, we don't have to say a thing, we just shoot."
Tucker "So if we were in a bank and some guy came in with a gun and held up the teller, you could just walk up behind him and do a contact shot to the base of his skull, no warning? Just fucking smoke him?"
Agent Jones "Oh yeah. As long as we don't endanger the civilian, sure."
Tucker "Have you ever done this?"
Agent Jones "No, never shot anyone. I mostly do white collar stuff."
Tucker "Does this ever cross your mind, that at any moment someone could commit a violent crime in front of you, and you could kill them without even warning them first?"
Agent Jones "You think I don't wish for that every single day of my life?"

Now *this* was the type of person that deserved to sit next to me. I decided to tell him the part of "The Austin Road Trip Story" where I shit the lobby, and he loved it. He came back with this one about his exploits with the US Border Patrol:

Agent Jones "I thought I was bad ass until I hung out with those guys. They're unbelievable. One time I was out with them right at the border. There is a big fence with concertina wire and what not all along this stretch, but the Coyotes had cut a hole in it—"

Tucker "What is a Coyote?"

Agent Jones "They are the guys who smuggle illegals back and forth over the border. Anyway, the Coyote was smuggling about a hundred Tonks through the hole, and—"

Tucker "What is a Tonk?"

Agent Jones "Oh—that's what Border Patrol calls illegal immigrants who have made it into the US. They can't call them 'wetbacks' or 'spicks' because obviously those are racially charged names, and 'Mexican' isn't accurate since a lot of illegals are not from Mexico, so they say 'Tonk.'"

Tucker "Why Tonk?"

Agent Jones "That's the sound it makes when you hit them on the head with a Maglite."

Tucker "HO-LEE-SHIT."

Agent Jones "It's messed up, I know. I told you, those guys are nuts. Anyway, so there we are, four trucks on this hill like 200 yards from the hole in the fence. We are totally blacked out, wearing night vision goggles and we can clearly see the Coyote hustling about a hundred Tonks through the fence. The Border Patrol guys wait until all of them are through the hole and about 50 yards into our side, when all four trucks simultaneously turn on all their spot lights and sirens. Of course, the Tonks shit themselves and bust ass back to the border . . . and in the darkness, they all run right into the concertina wire. It was a fucking mess. Some of them did not make it."

Tucker "You have to be kidding me."

Agent Jones "Nope. You think our force continuum is loose? These guys shoot anything they want. You should see their situation reports for deaths. They'll take out guys with rifles at 100 yards and write in the report, 'Subject was threatening agent with a rock.' It's a joke."

I got off the plane and parted ways with Agent Jones, who was officially in my Awesome Guy Hall of Fame. Riding a great buzz, basking in my ingeniously slick maneuvering into first class, and having just heard some hilarious stories about disproportionate and illegal acts of violence, I headed to the gate for my Nantucket connection in a great fucking mood.

Then karma decided that my day was going too well and kicked me in the nuts. My flight to Nantucket was canceled, stranding me in the Newark airport for six hours. Not to be outdone by the whims of karma, fate then decided to reroute me through Boston. This meant I would get into Nantucket at like midnight instead of 7pm, and the Nantucket bars close at 1am. Fuck you, karma. And fuck you too, fate.

I finally got to Boston and found my way to the right terminal just as they'd begun the boarding process. They opened the gate doors, but instead of going down a jetway onto a real plane, we took a flight of stairs down onto the tarmac. We were outside, on the fucking runway, with all these huge jets around us. But we weren't getting on one of those.

Sitting right there in front of me was the smallest joke of a plane I had ever seen. It was like I was in an episode of "Wings" or something. This is what it looked like:

Photo: Stinkie Pinkie

Look at that fucking thing. LOOK AT IT. It's a fucking short bus with wings, and I was about to spend 45 minutes in it, flying over water? Great.

I turned to the guy next to me, "This is a funny prank, but where is the real plane? This is some kid's model airplane or something."

He gave me a look of complete disdain and turned away. Obviously this guy didn't realize that he was beneath me. I was about to enlighten him, when one of the ground crew guys came up and looked at the five of us like we were cattle at auction. He kinda furrowed his brow:

"Alright, we have to assign seats to distribute passengers according to weight," then he points to me, "You're in the front."

I nearly had to crawl to get through the tiny door into the plane; I felt like I was in the play area at McDonald's. I sat in the front seat, and the pilot was literally right in front of me. My sense of cockpit security vanished as I realized I could just reach up and choke the pilot to death without even leaving my seat. The ground crew guy popped his head in:

Ground crew "No man, the very front. Next to the pilot."
Tucker "WHAT?"
Pilot "Yeah, it's fine. Come on up."
Tucker "You can't be serious. You want me to co-pilot? A PLANE?"
Pilot "No. Just sit here. We need the smallest person in this seat."

It took me about ten minutes to calm down. Then, once I re-attached my nutsack, I realized how fucking cool this was. I was sitting in the co-pilot seat. The controls were right there in front of me! The throttle, the altimeter, the airspeed indicator, the suction gauge, the tachometer, everything. Even the goddamn co-pilot control wheel! I could just grab the thing. In fact, that is exactly what I did.

Pilot "No no, you don't want to do that."
Tucker "I was just trying to be helpful."

After awhile, my fear completely evaporated, and I was more curious than anything else. I've never flown a plane, but I have played a lot of flight simulator games, so I had a good idea of what some of the controls actually did. I asked the pilot a few intermediate questions, so he'd know I wasn't a total assclown. Then I asked him:

Tucker "Can I fly the plane? You know, when we are up in the air? Like take the controls?"
Pilot "Sure. That's fine."
Tucker "And can I switch on the marker beacon when we get there? It's this button, I remember from Microsoft Flight Simulator. That's my favorite part, night carrier landings."
Pilot "Sure, OK."
Tucker "WOO-HOO! Alright, you be Maverick and I'll be Goose. It'll be great!"
Pilot "Uh . . . OK."
Tucker "Did you like that movie? You know, being a pilot and all?"
Pilot "Yeah, it was pretty good."
Tucker "The Defense Department regrets to inform you that your sons are dead because they were stupid!"

He kinda gave me this look and put his earphones on, which I guess was my cue to shut the fuck up. Once we were up in the air and cruising, he gave me the nod and I took the wheel. It was loud as shit in there, so I had to yell.

Tucker "I FEEL THE NEED, THE NEED FOR SPEED!"

As I yelled, I kinda shook the controls accidentally, the plane wobbled slightly, and he immediately took back the controls. Seconds after it began, my career as a pilot unceremoniously ended.

We came up on the island, and it was covered with clouds; I couldn't see shit. All of a sudden, a line of lights popped up, right down the middle of the runway, but I could barely see it through the clouds. He motioned for me to press the marker beacon button, but told me to wait for his signal. We went into the clouds, and the whole fucking plane whited out. I couldn't see anything. We started bouncing around, and even though we were only in there for about five seconds, it seemed like forever. As we started to come out the bottom, he motioned for me to hit the beacon, and almost out of nowhere, the entire runway lit up. It was awesome.

That is probably the closest I'll ever come to flying a jet or doing a night aircraft carrier landing, and it was fucking thrilling. I can only imagine what it's like flying a real jet. No wonder pilots are so arrogant. If I did that for a living, you'd have a hard time convincing me I wasn't a minor deity.

At Chevy's family house in Nantucket, his mom put the four of us in the guest house behind the main house. This "guest" house was loaded with antiques and knickknacks; it looked like a fucking Restoration Hardware or something. Chevy's mom is very nice, but a total uppity society woman, very prim and proper. So of course, I can't help myself:

Tucker "You have a very nice guest house, Mrs. Chevy."
Mrs. Chevy "Thank you, Tucker."
Tucker "It must have taken your family forever to steal all this stuff."
Mrs. Chevy "Excuse me?"

Minus Mom, we went out drinking in Nantucket. Let me give you some advice: If you haven't ever been there, do not go. It fucking sucks. Wait, I am being hasty. There are some people who should go to Nantucket:

• If you are a wanna-be Kennedy with your perfectly windswept hair and Revos you never take off because you spent the day clamming in the North Face vest you also never take off because you are just so fucking authentic New England, then you will love Nantucket.

• If you are pompous douche who inherited his money from Mommy and Daddy, and have no personality and no motivation to actually do anything with your life except be a sheep in your pink polo shirts, drink over-priced appletinis and hit on ugly girls because they are also sheep from rich families, then Nantucket is for you.

- Or if you are just old and rich and white and only want to be around other old rich white people, then Nantucket is heaven.

Here is a perfect example of what the island is like: Around 1:15am the first night we all headed to some late-night eatery. Chevy is a total prick, even worse than me, and he mouthed off to some typical Nantucket shit-bird. Nothing big, just stupid drunk talk that we all ignore.

This one guy, PoppedCollar, decided that he was not going to let Chevy get away with talking shit to him. But instead of confronting Chevy him-self, like a man would do if he had a problem, he went and got three of his friends, all bigger than him. These three friends got up in Chevy's face, but get this: PoppedCollar stood outside watching! He basically hired someone else to fight his fight! What a pussy. These are the "men" that hang out in Nantucket.

I was next to Dallas, one of Chevy's friends that I'd just met that week-end. Dallas is from Mississippi, played football at an SEC school, and is a total Southern guy, the type of guy who dips while he drinks. Awesome. I grabbed him:

Tucker "Dallas, we need to go help Chevy."

He kinda looked at me, and then looked at PoppedCollar, "No, hold on." He walked over to PoppedCollar.

Dallas "Let me ask you a question. Those yur friends in thar?"
PoppedCollar [acting like he is tough] "Yeah."
Dallas "Let me ask you another question: Do yew know howta fight?"

The way Dallas said it, even I was intimidated. You ever met one of those guys who, in a totally calm and composed way, can scare the shit out of you? Like an MMA fighter, or the fat Kardashian sister who married Lamar Odom? Dallas is like that. When he is serious, you can feel the vio-lence behind his calm. PoppedCollar's tough guy image dropped immedi-ately.

———————

PoppedCollar "Uh . . . no, not really."

Dallas [totally playing up his southern accent] "Have yew ever fawght someone from tha south bafour?"

PoppedCollar "Uhhhh . . ."

Dallas "Well, I'm an amacheur boxer, and I train for UFC-style fightin', and if a faight starts, I ken promise yew that I'm comin fer yew. Not yer buddies—YEW. Considerin' our backgrawnds, and my steel-toed boots, yew sure yew still wanna dew this?"

PoppedCollar "Uhhhh, no, I guess not."

Dallas "Well then go tell yer boys to back off, and we'll go our separate ways."

PoppedCollar "OK."

PoppedCollar walked right in there, pulled his boys away from Chevy and left.

Dallas [waves to them as they walk off] "Have a nice naight, y'all."

The next day, we went deep-sea fishing off the island. It was awesome. I caught like eight bluefish. Of course, the highlight of everyone else's day was another incident. I kept fucking up my casts, so the captain of the boat stood next to me to see what I was doing, and he said I didn't have my hands properly situated on the line. So he took my hand to reposition it, and then exclaimed:

Captain "Well damn there's the problem—look at your tiny hands. You can't even reach the line properly. Here, use the light tackle pole, that's small enough for you."

Thanks, asshole, I'm definitely not going to get shit for this for the rest of the weekend or anything.

We went to dinner that night with Chevy's parents, and like everything on Nantucket, it was pretty boring, unless you think it's just HILARIOUS that Dallas got the waiter to bring me a lobster fork for my entree. The only good part—to me—was when Chevy's mom got drunk and we goaded her into telling us stories about Chevy.

Mrs. Chevy "Oh you boys don't even know what a handful Chevy is. He just sits around all day, scratching himself so much you'd think our house was overrun with crabs."
Chevy "MOM!"
Mrs. Chevy "I don't have many stories about things he's done that you guys don't know. Besides, he doesn't tell me the real bad things, I just pay the bail bondsman and don't ask questions."
Tucker "He has to have done something he hasn't told us about."
Mrs. Chevy "Well . . . OH! Did he ever tell you about the summer he spent in Maui tagging whales?"

The whole table lost it, mainly because she didn't get the joke—she was actually talking about working with marine wildlife, not fucking fat girls.

All the guys kinda looked at me, expecting me to drop some hilariously subtle quip. If you are a football fan, you know how even though a great defensive back can catch anything not thrown to him, when the pass comes right at him he will freeze and drop it? Yep.

Tucker "Uhhh . . . CHEVY FUCKS FAT GIRLS!"

Great job, Tucker.

We went out drinking after dinner, and waded back into the sea of fuck-sticks that is the Nantucket social scene. I start talking to one girl, and somehow the discussion of penis size comes up.

Girl "Size doesn't matter in guys."
Tucker "I hear that a lot, but it's always in a consoling tone. I'm not buying it."
Girl "Really, it's not a big deal."
Tucker "Whatever, it's alright, I've found a way to get around it."

Girl [kinda suspicious of what I'm going to say, but still interested] "Oh, what's that?"

Tucker "Well, I always slide a ball point pen in the girl's pussy first, because the vagina will naturally constrict to fit the size of whatever is put in it. Then, when I put my dick in, it feels huge in comparison."

I was obviously kidding, and thought that was hilarious, but she was offended. And so were her friends. They sucked. Seriously, one of them looked like Snaggle Tooth from *Star Wars,* and the rest were rejects from the *Village of the Damned.* The best part: THEY HAD ATTITUDE! Nothing is more obnoxious than ugly rich girls who think they are hot. Thank you, but I'd rather pull my dick out by the root than talk to girls like that.

I think it all ended with this exchange, where one of the girls was bitching about some doucher ex-boyfriend of hers:

Girl [blah blah blah, my ex boyfriend sucked, blah blah blah, he is the worst person ever, etc, etc.]

Tucker "I'm sorry, hold on a minute. You dated this guy for like two years, right?"

Girl "Yeah."

Tucker "And in that time, you supported him and loved him and fucked him and did all this shit for him, right?"

Girl "Yeah."

Tucker "So if he sucks as much as you keep saying, and you STILL did all that stuff for him—doesn't that mean you suck more?"

She didn't want to talk to me after that.

I went to the bar to get another drink, and finally, like 45 minutes later, when the asshole bartender deigned to serve me, he informed me that they were out of vodka. OUT of vodka. What the fuck does that even mean in a bar, out of vodka?

I'd had enough. Enough of the dipshits, enough of the pompous idiots, enough of fighting off these tools to get into overcrowded places that sucked ass, I was just fed up. I walked out of the bar and into the street, looking around for some place that didn't suck.

Down the street, I saw a big crowd, and started walking in that direction. As I got closer, the girls out front looked a bit young, and then they started to look way too young, and then I was just weirded out, because there were clearly children hanging out at like 11:30 at night. What was going on?

Then I saw a kid with a blue lightning bolt painted on his forehead, dressed in a cape and holding a broomstick . . . holy shit, it was Friday, July 15th . . . this was a release party for the sixth Harry Potter book. This wasn't a bar; it was a bookstore. There were at least 100 kids of various ages and their parents hanging out here.

At this point, I had a decision to make. I could:

A. Leave immediately and go find a bar

B. Hang out and mess with the Harry Potter fans, or

C. Put on a cape, grab a wand and join them in pretending that we're wizards so we can vainly attempt to escape from the soul-crushing reality of our lives.

I stood and thought about it: What was going to maximize my utility tonight? There was only about an hour more of drinking left because this island sucked. I was not very drunk and wouldn't get to a good level in only an hour, so that was pretty much a sunk cost. There were not many girls on this island and the ones that were there sucked, plus the chances of finding one I liked that I could also pick up, all in the span of just an hour, were not great. And to be honest, I was going to buy a copy of the new Harry Potter book anyway . . .

Fuck it, Harry Potter it is.

———————

I got in line and bought my ticket at like 11:40, then stood outside under the huge tent with everyone else, waiting for the books to be passed out. As I looked around, I saw all kinds of people, not just little kids and parents. There were teenagers, young adults, old people, just about every demographic was represented, and tons of little kids. I started to get nervous. Like all grown men in the post-"To Catch A Predator" world, I am deathly afraid of even talking to little children.

So I kinda stood off to the side and covered my face with my hand. I looked ridiculous, so of course this little kid came up to me. She was dressed like Hermione. She couldn't have been more than 8, but her parents weren't anywhere that I could see.

Kid "What are you doing?"
Tucker "Where are your parents?"
Kid "Over there talking to Snape. Are you excited about the book?"
Tucker "Beyond ecstatic. I can barely contain my emotions."
Kid "I can't wait to find out what happens! They say someone dies, I wonder who it'll be."
Tucker "Didn't you hear? It's Ron that dies in this one."

A look of complete horror enveloped her face and her eyes started welling up with tears.

Tucker "NO NO NO—I'm just kidding. Totally kidding, please don't cry, Ron doesn't die, I'm just kidding."

She stopped her tears and her face went back to normal. I couldn't help myself:

Tucker "It's actually Hermione that dies."

She turned and ran off in tears. Oh well, she had to learn at some point that guys are assholes and will take advantage of female naiveté whenever possible. Better now, before she reaches puberty and starts dating.

———

I immediately moved to the other side of the tent and got in line. I didn't want to deal with her irate parents and I wanted to avoid being approached by any more unsupervised, underage girls. I have to deal with that shit enough in my regular life.

With like three minutes until they released the book, this nerd in front of me was getting all kinds of giddy. He was probably 23 or so, and had the typical huge nerd backpack that contained his every single possession. He kept turning left and right, hitting me with his backpack. It went on this for five minutes, constantly bumping into me, and not once recognizing it or moving or apologizing. Well, if he won't stop, then I'll stop him. I reached down (he was short) and grabbed his backpack, holding him still.

Nerd "HEY!! WHAT THE!!! HEY!!"

The nerd started flailing around like a turtle on its back. He was flailing his arms around and trying everything he could to reach me, but kept failing because his backpack was too unwieldy for him and he was an uncoordinated dork.

Tucker "Calm down. You need to stop hitting me with your backpack."
Nerd "HEY! GET OFF ME YOU SNOTTY-FACED HEAP OF PARROT DROPPINGS!"

I HATE dorks that quote Monty Python, so I decided to teach him a simple lesson: This was real life, not a delightful British comedy. I swept his legs, and he immediately crashed to the ground. I kinda laughed at him, thinking that this will shut him up. I mean come on, this kid was like 130 pounds, including his backpack. I could strangle him with a bread tie. If he tried to fight me, I'd hit him so hard he'd have to walk toward the light to ask Jesus what just happened.

But he struggled back to his feet, and got in my face, kinda chest bumping me in the process. I grabbed his shirt in a rage:

Tucker "DO YOU ACTUALLY WANT TO FIGHT ME? ARE YOU FUCKING INSANE? I SHIT BIGGER THAN YOU!"

Two "adults" got between us, and we both kinda looked at each other, realizing that everyone within earshot was now staring at us . . . and that we had become *those* guys . . . who started a fight . . . at a Harry Potter book party.

Oh man.

Someone working there handed me my book—a minute early I think—and I slinked off. I'm pretty sure even the little kids were making fun of me.

I got back to the house before everyone else, sat on the couch, and started reading. For real—it was 12:30am on a summer Saturday night in Nantucket, and I was reading Harry Potter, alone.

Everyone else stumbled in around 1:30am. Chevy and Dallas took one look at me, and of course went nuts:

Dallas "Are you reading Harry Potter?!?"
Chevy "YOU FUCKING NERD! THAT'S WHERE YOU WENT OFF TO? TO GET THE NEW HARRY POTTER BOOK! HOLY SHIT!!!"
Tucker "Reading about Quiddich is better than going out on this shitty island!"

Suddenly, the fourth guy in our group, Ralphie, got this awful look on his face.

Ralphie "I don't think the mussels are sitting right."

We broke down laughing as he ran to the bathroom and started puking. But this wasn't normal puke. The dude was like 130 decibels:

"BBLLLAAAAAAAAAAAAAAAAHHHHHHHHHHHHH!!"

He was so loud, it was ridiculous. It was like the dude was trying to scream the vomit out of him. And he was giving commentary the whole time. Like a pukey, disoriented Gus Johnson:

"OH SHIT!!! BLLLLLLLLLLAAAAAAAAAAAHHHHHHH!!!!!!
HERE IT COMES!!! BLLLLLLLLLLAAAAAAAAAAAAHHHHHHH!!!!!!
WHAT THE FUCK BLLLLLLLAAAAAAAAAAAAAAAAAHHHHHH!!"

He finally stopped, and we tried to open the door, but it was locked.

Chevy "Ralphie . . . you OK?"
Ralphie "Yeah. Do you have a plunger?"
Chevy "I don't know. If we do, it's in there."

We hear Ralphie searching around, knocking stuff over, getting frustrated.

Ralphie "I don't believe it! All the money your family has, and they don't have a plunger!"
Chevy "I don't think anyone has ever stopped up a toilet from puke before."

This of course was high comedy. But it got better. Once Ralphie felt he had cleaned up the bathroom enough to come out . . . he couldn't.

Ralphie "Chevy, why won't the bathroom door open?"
Chevy "You're the one who locked it!"
Ralphie "It won't open! I can't get the lock undone!"

What kind of idiot locks himself IN the bathroom? There is no 24-hour locksmith in Nantucket; the earliest he could come to free Ralphie was the next day.

Ralphie "I'm going to kick the door down!"
Chevy "NO! This is the original woodwork! The door is like a hundred and fifty years old! My mom will kill me!"

Ralphie "This is the guest bathroom in the guest house! She'll never know!"

Chevy "Are you kidding? As soon as we leave she's going through this place with a fine tooth comb."

Ralphie "What do you want me to do Chevy, sleep in the fucking tub??"

Chevy "Hold on, lemme think!"

Ralphie "Don't think, you're a fucking idiot!"

They tried the lock for another hour or so, but eventually Ralphie just gave up and slept in the tub.

That was pretty much the entire weekend. No fucking, barely any drinking, no crazy antics. Just me getting in a fight . . . at a children's book party. And Nantucket sucks.

Fuck the fucking
Headboard

Occurred, April, 2005

If you read my first book you probably remember "The Midland Story," where I hung out in Midland, Texas with my friend Doug and his redneck friends. The story ends with me and Doug helping Cliff bury his dead goats.

Well, right after that incident, literally that night, I drove to Dallas because the next day I was flying out of the most inconvenient airport on earth, DFW. There was a girl in Dallas who I'd fucked a few times before, and she wanted to do it again. We met at a bar first:

Her "What'd you do today?"
Tucker "Buried some dead goats."
Her "No you didn't."
Tucker "Smell my hands."

I hadn't washed my hands yet, and they stank like rotten animal.

Her "Oh my God, that is so disgusting. You are gross!"
Tucker "Whatever, you're still fucking me, so quiet down."
Her "You know, you don't have one charming bone in your body."
Tucker "Yes I do, it's right here." I pointed to my crotch.
Her "Do you know why girls sleep with you? It's because—"
Tucker "I don't care why. They do and that's all that matters."

We eventually go back to my hotel and fuck. It starts out great as usual, and in her ecstasy she grabs the headboard. This is a Hampton Inn I think, so the furniture is not real well made, and this headboard was particularly bad. Worse than Ikea, but not quite as bad as the shit people leave on their corner for poor people to pick up. It wasn't even attached to the bed frame—it was actually mounted to the wall instead. She dislodged the headboard when she grabbed it, and then would not shut the fuck up about it. It felt like fucking a play-by-play announcer.

Her "Oh my God, it's cracking."
Tucker [humping]
Her "I can feel it giving way."
Tucker [humping]
Her "I think it's going to break."
Tucker [humping]
Her "Oh my God, it's breaking right now!"
Tucker [humping]
Her "It's broken off! The headboard is broken off the wall! What do we do now!?!"
Tucker "Are we not fucking? Seriously, I have my dick in you, and you are worried about the FUCKING HEADBOARD???"

It didn't even fucking hit us; it just fell on the bed. To make sure she'd shut up and fuck, I pull out, drag her across the bed so we're two feet away and parallel to the head board—which is now sitting on the bed, propped against the wall— and start fucking there. Now she has to shut the fuck up about the fucking headboard, right?

Nope. We get back to fucking, full on coitus, not touching the headboard, the headboard not moving, and STILL she wouldn't stop. Over the course of their entire careers, I don't think headboard manufacturers talk about headboards as much as this girl did during five minutes of sex.

Her "Do you think I broke the headboard?"
Tucker [humping]
Her "Are we going to have to pay to fix the headboard if it's broken?"
Tucker [humping]

Her "Why do you think the headboard fell?"
Tucker [humping]
Her "I wonder what kind of wood it is? What do you think? Cherry? Teak?"
Tucker [humping]
Her "Do you think Headboard would make a good name for a child?"
Tucker [humping]
Her "Headboard! Headboard! Headboard! Headboard! Headboard!"
Tucker [humping]
Her "You can take my life, but you can never take, my HEEEEAAAAAD BOOOOOAAAAARRRRRRRRRRDD!"

OK, I made up those last few. It's not like I was listening to her, I was busy trying to get the white goo to shoot out of my dick. All I know is she was definitely babbling incessantly about the headboard for a preposterous and unreasonable amount of time. It was worse than listening to Dick Vitale fawn over a Duke/UNC game.

There I was, lying on top of her, penis inside her vagina, trying to fuck, and I can't because this girl will not shut up about the headboard. I didn't know what else I could do, so I bit her on the nose. Not hard or anything, but enough to get her attention.

Her "OWW! Why did you bite my nose?"
Tucker "BECAUSE YOU WON'T SHUT THE FUCK UP ABOUT THE FUCKING HEADBOARD!"
Her "What if it breaks or falls again?!"
Tucker "IT'S SITTING ON THE BED! WHERE IS IT GOING TO FALL FROM?!"
Her "I DON'T KNOW!"

I got up and went into the bathroom to cool off. I can't recall any time in my life that a girl has ever made me so angry as I was having sex. Really, I can't. Girls have made me happy, anguished, terrorized, affectionate, and depressed during sex, but never angry. Think about it—how can someone even piss you off AS YOU ARE FUCKING?

I come back from the bathroom, relatively calm and settled and ready to try again . . . to find her balled up on the bed, crying her eyes out. No really, she was in hysterical tears.

Tucker "Why are you crying?"
Her "You bit me on the nose and the headboard is broken!!"

If Ashton Kutcher had busted into the room with cameras and told me I was Punk'd, it would have made more sense than what was actually happening. Her actions were just not a reasonable or rational response to the events of the night. I was flummoxed. I had no idea how to deal with a girl who was inconsolably bawling because the headboard fell off the wall at a cheap hotel. This is just not part of any reality I understand.

I didn't know what to do, so I just started laughing. This only made her more upset, and she started screaming at me.

Her "OH!! YOU ARE SO COOL, YOU ARE TUCKER MAX THE FUCK-ING ASSHOLE!"
Tucker "That is the first thing you've said in 30 minutes that hasn't been about the headboard."
Her "FUCK YOU!"
Tucker "And that would be the second thing."
Her "Yeah, you are so cool."

She starts putting on her clothes, still crying.

Tucker "I mean seriously—is this happening right now? You are crying because I got mad that you wouldn't stop talking about the headboard during sex. When does this start making sense?"

She collects her things and goes to the door.

Tucker "You want to take the headboard with you? You can have it if you want."
Her "FUCK YOU AND FUCK THE FUCKING HEADBOARD!!"

———————

THE JUNIOR STORIES

I have a lot of friends with funny, ridiculous and crazy stories. SlingBlade is the funniest person I know, and Hate entertains me the most, but they don't have the best stories. That would be Junior. If you read *IHTSBIH,* you remember him from "The Vegas Story." That was a pretty crazy weekend in my life—but it probably wouldn't make it into the book about *his* life.

That book is up to him to write. In the meantime, I have a few good stories that involve both of us:

LA SUCKS

Occurred, Summer 2000

Here is how I described Junior in "The Vegas Story" in *IHTSBIH:*

"Junior is 5'9", well built, half-Italian half-Arabic, with light green eyes and olive skin. He's got that 'dark with light eyes' look that women lose their shit over. I knew Junior from Florida, where he used to work for my father. We became friends because he is one of the few people I've ever met in my life who not only does better with women that I do—WAY better, actually—but simply put, he can not only keep up with me, he can exceed me at times. Not many people can."

During the summer of 2000, between my 2L and 3L years at Duke Law School, I was fired from my first job as a lawyer at Fenwick & West in

Palo Alto (that story is told in "The Infamous Charity Auction Debacle" in *IHTSBIH*). Considering that it happened only three weeks into the summer, I had quite a bit of time to kill until my final year of law school started in the fall. After a few weeks of hanging out in San Francisco and getting drunk every night with SlingBlade, I decided to go hang out with Junior, who was living in LA. He shared this shitty two-bedroom apartment in Santa Monica with his cousin Amir, but it had a huge living room and two sofas, so I just set up shop on one of them.

The very first day I get there, at 2:00 in the afternoon, Junior and I start drinking. By 2:15, we start drinking heavily. Junior has a gambling problem, and the next thing I know we're watching some random horse races on channel 426, calling up an offshore book, trying to make bets on the races. We get through with two races left, and Junior and I make about 30 of the most idiotically complex bets possible. We're triple boxing trifectas, double boxing exactas, I'm making stuff up about buying put options on our bets—it was sweet, drunken bedlam.

At the end of the two races, the living room walls are coated with the beer we sloshed around while cheering for our horses. Except that we have no idea who we actually bet on. Junior calls up the book—we're up like $250!

Of course, we hoot and holler and celebrate like we've just won the fucking Powerball. This sets off a feeding frenzy. I pour more alcohol and Junior goes onto the book's website so we can take the $250 and play virtual table games. We begin recklessly betting money on anything and everything possible: roulette, baseball games, blackjack. In Vegas, I would never split 10s against a 6. On the internet? We did it TWICE. AND WON! Fuck the rules! It's not like it's real money anyway. It's an internet casino! We are screaming and drinking, jumping up and down, sloshing vodka all around his apartment. It's not even six o'clock.

Tucker "Dude, look at us: we are GROWN MEN. We are ADULTS, and we have done nothing today but gamble and drink!"
Junior "I know! It's awesome!"

The funny thing is that we consistently won; we finished up about $500 for the day. It's a gambling truth—if you don't care about the result and just have fun, you always do better than if you're trying hard.

His cousin Amir comes home at some point, looks at the scene, sighs, and says, "The sad part is, he's like this even when you aren't here."

This was basically my first time in LA, so Junior and Amir took me out drinking on Sunset strip. We ended up at a famous bar called Dubliner (which is now closed), and after about an hour or two there, I came to a conclusion that would basically never change, even after I lived in LA for two years: Most people in LA are soulless. I don't mean that they are evil or bad people necessarily (though many are); I mean that with the vast majority of LA people I met that night (and since), there was no "there" in there. They were nothing more than empty shells of human beings, devoid of emotional content, empathy, or substance of any sort.

Tucker "Junior . . . these people are awful."
Junior "Yeah, I know. Welcome to LA."

This is how bad it was—the one girl I met that night who seemed to have the most human traits and maybe had a soul, was Eastern European! If you know anything about Eastern European girls, you're laughing your ass off right now. This was 2000—pre 9/11—back when you could be reasonably sure that every girl you met in America from an ex-Soviet Bloc country had fucked at least 500 syphilitic Russians just for a spot in the shipping container bound for America.

I still could have dealt with that, maybe, if she didn't fucking smell. No, I don't think you understand. I'm not talking about that potent, hormonal musk you get from a race of hirsute, forest-dwelling ethnic cleansers. This bitch stank like a fucking homeless person. The sad part is, she was so hot and everyone else in this LA bar was so bad, I STILL would have hung in there. But what finally broke the straw for me was her breath. It could have melted steel. I was afraid to even let her blow me—I wasn't about to let whatever was causing that smell to touch my penis.

This bar was not a total loss, because they had a huge promotional inflatable Dewar's bottle. In the absence of humans to interact with and girls to put my penis in, my next favorite thing to do is to steal worthless shit. I decided the Dewar's bottle was coming home with me. Junior and I went off into a corner and concocted an elaborate plan. It consisted of me grabbing it, then running out of the bar.

Thankfully Junior can charm the habit off a pissed-off nun. He and Amir engaged the bouncers in conversation long enough to distract their focus and give me the time to turn the corner and get away. I waited for them to meet me at the car, but after like ten minutes I got frustrated and drove around the block to go pick them up.

I pull up to a scene from *The Warriors*. Junior, now by himself, is squared off against four guys who are all swinging at him and trying their best to kick his ass. I debate driving up on the sidewalk to save him, then realize that not only am I not Jason Statham, but I would run over Junior in the process. I consider getting out of the car, but two on four isn't much better than one on four. So I start honking. That distracts the dudes just long enough for Junior to jump in the car and for me to step on the accelerator.

Tucker "WHAT THE FUCK HAPPENED!?!? They fought you over an inflatable liquor bottle? Really?"
Junior "No, we were outside talking to the bouncers, and fucking Amir grabbed some girl's ass, and the guys she came with all jumped me."
Tucker "Where is Amir? Did he get knocked out?"
Junior "NO!! HE GOT BEHIND ME AND THEN FUCKING RAN OFF AND LEFT ME TO FIGHT THEM BY MYSELF!!"

Junior was pissed. I think he wanted to kick Amir's ass for starting this shit and then running off, but Amir is not only his cousin, he's also just little. Junior decided to take his anger out on the guys who jumped him—sort of. He told me to circle the block and come back outside the club. He'd seen what kind of car the two guys with the girl drove up in, and he was determined to get revenge on it. Think about this for a minute—his plan was to drive around in LA, looking for a random car. Don Quixote has formulated better revenge plans. We drove around for a fucking hour as I mocked him, but then, lo and behold—we found it!

Junior pulled up next to it, popped his trunk, pulled out a golf club, then jumped on top of the car and started smashing his golf club into the window. It was like watching a fraternity destroy an old car with sledge-hammers for charity. Except this was a new Mercedes, and the world's orphans were going to be just as broke and hungry as they were yesterday.

By the time he got back to the car, he was sweating profusely and laughing his ass off. And the iron he used was FUCKED up. It was a parody of a golf club.

Tucker "Dude, you just destroyed your club."
Junior "I can't hit my 4-iron straight anyway."

We decided to pick up some beer at the 7–11 and go back to his place to gamble more. I crack the first one before we even get in the car. I immediately spit it out. Junior tries one, and agrees—it's skunked. I look at the "Born On" label—it's like six months expired. I take the beer back in to return it. Unfortunately, the dude behind the register is an FOB Indian, and this turns into a whole fucking debacle:

Tucker "I want to return this beer, it's bad."
Indian "No bad. Beer fine. I see you drink."
Tucker "It's expired, you know, like milk does."
Indian "Is not milk!"
Tucker "I know it's not milk motherfucker! But it is expired, like milk does!"
Indian "No! No! Is NOT milk!"
Tucker "You're fucking killing me Apu—look at the fucking label!! The beer is skunked!"

It went back and forth like this for five minutes. He refused to give me my money back or let me exchange the beer, and I was too drunk to cogently explain my position to someone who learned English from watching game shows. Eventually I gave up and left. I think I may have smashed one of the bottles on the floor in anger, but since I paid for it already, I assume the clerk was OK with it.

Thankfully, we knew Amir had another bottle of vodka stashed in his room at their place, so we drank that. It seemed like a fair trade, considering he sexually assaulted a girl and then left his cousin to deal with the consequences.

We started gambling again and got HAMMERED, again. We'd already been drinking all day; this just put us over the top. At some point I went to take a dump, and I have no idea why, but Junior decided that this meant he should open the window of his second floor apartment and yell out at the top of his lungs.

"WOOOOOOOOOOO! WOOOOOOOOOOO! WOOOOOOOOOOO!"

He wasn't even saying anything; it was just a primal, drunken scream of triumph, repeated over and over again, like a train whistle. When I finally came out of the bathroom he still hadn't stopped.

Tucker "Junior, what the HELL are you doing?!?"

He burst out laughing. He looked like a pothead watching "Looney Tunes". We immediately went back online, and it was only a matter of time before we won big again. Junior went to the window and started yelling again.

Junior "WOOOOOOOOOOO! WOOOOOOOOOOO! WOOOOOOOOOOO!"

This time he wouldn't stop for anything. He wasn't even responding to my cursing at him. I looked around the apartment for something that might break his fixation, like you'd try with a tired baby. I found an easel over by the front door (it was Amir's).

I picked it up, grabbed it by the legs, and started smashing it over Junior's back as he leaned out the window. Junior is a strong dude, and this was not a very well made easel, so it shattered into a million little pieces. We laughed our asses off at this as we chucked the wood around the apartment and out the window.

Junior "WOOOOOOOOOOO! WOOOOOOOOOO! WOOOOOOOOOOOO!"

Still, Junior kept yelling. I threw water on him. This cracked him up for about five seconds, then he started yelling again. I had no idea how to stop him, and he went on and on. Mind you—it was now 4am.

All of the sudden, this blond master-race looking guy appeared on the sidewalk below Junior's apartment. He looked like a henchman from *Die Hard.* In the most heavily-accented Hans & Franz tone you can imagine, he looks up at Junior and yells:

German "Mahn, vhat ze hell mahn?!? Ahr you creh-zy??"

I laughed so hard I almost puked. Junior laughed so hard, he did puke. He lurched outside, threw up on the landing, and then fell down the stairs. I think the German guy thought Junior was coming to fight him, because he ran off. This made me laugh so hard, I ended up having to piss in a potted plant because I couldn't make it to the bathroom.

The next thing I remember is waking up. More specifically, being woken up by Junior shaking me violently. It had to be noon at least. I was passed out on the sofa. The TV was still on, blasting horse races. The apartment looked like a trailer park after a tornado. Junior looked as confused as I've ever seen him.

Junior "Tucker—why am I covered in bruises??"

JUNIOR AND THE FRENCH WHORE

Occurred, Summer 2000

During the period I visited him in LA, Junior was quasi-dating this French girl he met at a strip club down there; I think it was Jumbo's Clown Room. Naturally, he took me to meet her for the first time while she was working. Hey, if you're gonna meet your friend's special someone, she might as well be topless, right? She came out on stage, and I have to admit: She was stunningly hot. Perfect body, perfect tits, like she was carved out of pink marble. I might have even been a little bit envious.

Then she sat down to talk.

FrenchWhore "Allo June-ya!"

Her accent was so preposterous, I honestly thought she was kidding at first, that she was mocking the way French people talk.

[Read her dialogue in the most cartoonish, ridiculous, Pepe-Le-Pew-style French voice you can imagine in your head. Seriously, that's what she sounded like.]

Tucker "Do you have any hot friends for me to hook up with?"
FrenchWhore "Ook up? What does thees mean?"
Tucker "You know, boom boom sexy? Me love you long time?"
FrenchWhore "Boom boom sexy? What does thees mean?"
Tucker "Sex. Fucking. I know you do that."
FrenchWhore "Ooh yes, I like zah sex."
Tucker "Right, I know that. How about someone who wants to like the sex with me."
FrenchWhore "Noh, I only have zah sex weeth June-ya."
Tucker "Dude—is she kidding with this shit?"

Nope. She's just a fucking retarded frog.

I was astonished by what a colossal moron this girl was. We were sitting in a strip club, IN LOS ANGELES, and she was so dumb she stood out among the other spectacularly stupid whores. That's so stupid, it's an achievement. People get Wikipedia pages for less.

Tucker "How do you deal with this girl? I mean—what do you guys talk about?"
Junior "We don't talk much."

Maybe I'm being unfair to her. Maybe her English was so comically bad, it was just the language barrier that was preventing me from seeing her subtle and nuanced genius . . . AHHAHAHAHAHAHHAHAHA!!

Here, judge for yourself. These are some of the exchanges I can remember:

Tucker "So what do you think of the Germans?"
FrenchWhore "I like Germahny."
Tucker "You aren't mad that they invaded you and stole all your croissants and snails?"
FrenchWhore "Noh. Zhat was befohr I was born."
Tucker "Really? So if I rape you and steal all your shit, then your kids should be cool with it?"
FrenchWhore "I do not have children."

Tucker "Do you wear deodorant?"
FrenchWhore "Dehodorant, yes."
Tucker "Isn't that how you shower? By just spraying perfume on? That's how the French bathe, right?"
FrenchWhore "Noh. We use shower, like you."
Tucker "Well then why do French people smell?"
FrenchWhore "Who smells?"

Tucker "How long have you been in America?"
FrenchWhore "A year, I sink."

Tucker "So why don't you speak better English?"

FrenchWhore "I try to. It es hard, English."

Tucker "I don't understand, I thought all French kids learned English in school."

FrenchWhore "Yes, we do."

Tucker "So what happened to you? You were too busy smoking cigarettes and eating baguettes to pay attention?"

FrenchWhore "It es very hard for me."

Tucker "So you have a bunch of problems with the language, yet decide to come here to live? Makes total sense."

Tucker "What's the French word for "hard work"?

FrenchWhore "I don't understand zis."

Tucker "Exactly. I bet you know the word for 'strike' and 'smelly cheese' though don't you?"

The next day she came over to Junior's apartment to hang out. She had this annoying little yippy dog with her named "Killer." It was ridiculously undisciplined and paid no attention to anything she said. All she did was chase the dog around the apartment, saying its name in her cartoonish French accent.

FrenchWhore "Kee-lah, Kee-lah, no Kee-lah, come here Kee-lah."

I love dogs and I love hot girls, but this stupid frog and her yippy dog annoyed me so much, I nearly curb-stomped her and punted that dog out the window. Junior was amused by my anger, but it was no match against perfect French titties. It wasn't long before he got horny, took her into his room and started fucking her. Super. Now she'll smell like sweat, perfume, AND sex.

A few minutes later, Junior comes out of the bedroom with a disgusted look on his face. FrenchWhore follows behind, looking very sad.

FrenchWhore "I sorry. I eat Mexican food for lunch."

Junior sits there looking pissed off and ignoring her for an hour. I am confused, but don't really care enough to ask. She finally gets the hint, and, after chasing "Kee-Lah" around for ten minutes and finally catching him, she leaves.

Tucker "So? What happened?"
Junior "Well, right in the middle of sex I hear this 'psssssssssssssssstttt' noise. She stops and says, 'Oh no . . . I fhar-TED.' And then I smell the most rancid fart smell I've ever smelt. Tucker, this wasn't a fart. This was a felony. It smelled so bad I gagged. I became totally flaccid dude. I just rolled off her and lay there, waiting for the smell to go away. But it wouldn't. I was disgusted. She lay next to me for about two minutes, not saying anything. Then—get this—with the stink still choking the life out of me, she turns towards me, gently puts her hand on my shoulder, and whispers in my ear, 'What's wrong? You no think I'm sexy?'"

To this day, whenever a girl does something disgusting in our presence, Junior and I will say in the thickest French accent we can muster, 'What's wrong? You no think I'm sexy?'"

About a week later, she comes over again and the three of us are hanging out in his living room watching TV. Junior decides he wants a Gatorade, so he says he's going to 7–11, and asks us if we want anything. Neither I nor FrenchWhore want anything, so he heads off by himself. [FYI—This isn't weird behavior from Junior at all, the dude has serious ADD and goes to 7–11 like five times a day.]

About thirty minutes pass, which is a bit long for Junior to be gone. Then my phone rings: It's Junior.

Junior "Are you in the living room?"
Tucker "Yeah of course."
Junior "Go in the bathroom and shut the door."

Oh no. This is going to be bad.

Tucker "OK, I'm in here. What's up?"

Junior "I need you to help me out."

Tucker "What's wrong, you OK?"

Junior "Oh yeah, yeah—I met a hot girl at 7–11, I'm going back to her place. I need you to cover for me with FrenchWhore."

Tucker "WHAT? Is this a joke?"

Junior "I'm totally serious, you gotta help me out."

Tucker "You're going home with a girl you met at the 7–11? What the fuck? Did your eyes meet over the corndogs and you knew it was true love?"

Junior "AHHAHAHAHAHA—no, but that's close. We were both looking at the wine, and I started talking to her about it, and now I'm following her to her place."

Tucker "You have to be kidding. What am I supposed to tell this stupid frog?"

Junior "I don't know, just tell her I went to jail or something."

Tucker "Tell her you went to jail? She doesn't even speak English!!"

Junior "Come on man, just handle it. Fuck her if you want, I don't care. I'm at the girl's place now."

Tucker "I'm not fucking a farting frog! . . . Hello . . . Hello! . . . YOU FUCK-ING ASSHOLE!"

Only Junior would seal up a girl over the 7–11 wine display. What did they talk about, the great nose on that new white zin? I have no idea what to do . . . so I sit on the toilet and take a dump. Halfway through pooping, I have a striking thought: Why do I care about lying to this girl? I'm not fucking her. Plus, this is a blessing in disguise—I'll have the apartment to myself all night. And bonus: I won't have to smell her awful floral perfume mixed with Junior's sperm! Everyone wins!

Tucker "Hey, that was Junior on the phone. He got arrested. He's in jail now."

FrenchWhore "Jail?"

Tucker "Prison. You know," and I pantomime putting my hands on bars in front of me, like I'm in jail, "Behind bars." She is truly confused.

FrenchWhore "Prison? Why he go to prison at the 7–11?"

Tucker "No, he got arrested at the 7–11. Now he's in prison. You know, police," and for some strange reason, I make a police siren sound, and spin my hands above my head, trying to imitate a police car.

FrenchWhore "Police? Why police?"

Tucker "I don't know, I wasn't there. I was here with you. Remember?"

FrenchWhore "Why June-ya go with police?"

Instead of trying to help her figure this out, I make the mistake of being a smartass.

Tucker "Because he's a wanted criminal. He's been on the run for years. Very bad man. Kills puppies."

FrenchWhore "What does zes mean, on ze run?"

Tucker "He's a criminal. A bad man. He kicks babies in the mouth and then steals their candy."

FrenchWhore "He keeck za babies? What does zes mean?"

I didn't know what to do, so I took the remote and smashed her skull with it. Just kidding. I wish. I actually just turned the TV volume way up. She looked at me confused, but I ignored her. This worked for about five minutes.

FrenchyWhore "Where is June-ya?"

Tucker "He's dead. He died in a car wreck."

FrenchyWhore "He's dead? I don't understand. I thought he go with police."

Tucker "Yeah, I think the cops killed him."

She asked me where Junior was at least four more times. She even tried calling him, but he didn't answer. After some interminable amount of time, she finally got the hint, and left.

Not long after that, I met some girl and I basically lived at her place for two weeks, doing nothing but eating her food and shooting loads in her. The next time I went over to Junior's, I asked him:

Tucker "Where is my favorite stinky whore, I haven't seen her for awhile."

Junior "You aren't going to believe this. Hold on, you have to hear it—"

Junior cues up his voicemail, and hands me the phone. I can hear her nasally, annoying accent before I even get the phone to my ear:

FrenchWhore "Allo June-ya, I sorry I no you call you back, but zee immigration police, they come and take me to zee jail. I am back now. You want me to come ova?"

Eventually Junior stops fucking her altogether and moves on to some other broken whore he met in line at an El Pollo Loco talking about the finer points of poultry brining. I don't fucking know.

Of course that wasn't *really* the end of Frenchie the Fungal Skank. About six months later, when I was back at law school, I get a call from Junior. He is laughing so hard he can barely talk. I eventually get the story out of him:

Amir was dating a girl who worked for some porn company. Every week she would bring him old, leftover porn VHS tapes lying around their office. You have to remember, this was 2000—not only when people still had VHS tapes, but before internet video took off and pretty much all internet porn became free (yes, it sucked, and I can't wait to tell my grandkids about how, back in the days before limitless free porn, I had to walk uphill through the snow just to buy porn on a VHS tape).

Well, one day Amir was watching one of them, and saw something he couldn't believe: The FrenchWhore, doing a porn movie. Junior didn't believe it at first, but then saw the butterfly tattoo on her left hip. It was her.

We laughed about this for hours. She had never EVER talked about doing porn. Junior had even asked her about it. She swore that her only job was working at Jumbo's Clown Room and running the massage table she put up every weekend on Venice Beach (if you lived around there during that time, she was the hot French girl who called herself "Beauty and the Beast" and would give massages on the boardwalk with her dog). The best part was the actual porn itself:

Junior "She was fucking like a goddamn acrobat in this thing. She looked like she really knew how to fuck. But she SUCKED in bed with me. She was like a dead fish. That's why I stopped fucking her in the first place! She was terrible in bed!"

I was wrong. Apparently the French do know how to work. Hard.

HOW IRON CHEF MORIMOTO (AND JUNIOR) GOT ME KICKED OUT OF MY OWN CHARITY EVENT

Occurred, April 2005

If you like the Food Network, and you've only seen "Iron Chef America", I pity you. That show sucks. Maybe not if it were judged on its own, but I can't help but compare it to the show it was based on, the masterpiece that was the original Japanese version of the show called "Iron Chef." It is arguably the greatest reality show—and inarguably the greatest cooking show—in the history of TV.

There is so much to love about the show. You kinda have to watch it to understand, but the show opens with this preposterous made-up story about some rich guy who decides to spend his fortune to create a kitchen stadium where the greatest chefs in the world compete to create new dishes. Then he takes a huge bite out of a yellow pepper, I guess to drive home the point about what a fruit loop he is.

But the thing is—those motherfuckers can cook. I grew up in a restaurant family and I know and love food, and I would be transfixed by some of the amazing things these chefs came up with. There was Iron Chef French Hiroyuki Sakai, Iron Chef Japanese Roksaboru Machiba and Iron Chef Chinese Chen Kenichi, and all were masters who battled the greatest chefs in the world. But to me, there was one Iron Chef who stood above the rest:

The second Iron Chef Japanese, Masaharu Morimoto.

He is the guy who made Nobu in NYC the legendary restaurant that it is now. He is the guy who turned traditional Japanese food on its head; he basically invented the idea of haute cuisine Asian fusion. I have been watching Iron Chef Morimoto on TV for years, reveling at the masterpiece dishes he created on the fly, his recreations of traditional Japanese fare, and the fearlessness he showed in the face of the established Japanese food community who hated him for what they saw as an attack on tradition. This dude had fucking balls, and he won with style.

The notion of the celebrity chef is now common, but Iron Chef Morimoto laid the groundwork for all of them. Fuck these bullshit American TV chefs who are all style and no substance—Emeril Lagasse and Guy Fieri and all the rest of the fat worthless fucks who do nothing but pander to the cameras and dance like minstrels for the attention of idiots. They are just glorified cooks, not chefs. Morimoto is a master chef and an artist, who just happens to use food as his paints and the plate as his canvas. Plus, he's got real style. He's the first chef I've ever seen that made me think, "That dude is probably cool outside of a kitchen." The motherfucker cooked in a silver kimono for fuck's sake!

So you can imagine my excitement when, in 2004, I got this phone call:

Junior "You're not going to believe the restaurant that just hired me to be the general manager."
Tucker "McDonald's?"

Junior "Morimoto's in Philly. Your boy."
Tucker "Shut the fuck up!! That's amazing!!!"

I think I was more excited than Junior. It only took a few months before Morimoto and Junior were good friends. Junior has an amazing ability to get pretty much anyone to like him. I'm charismatic too, but in a self-centered way; Junior is more of a seducer. The dude makes you feel like he understands you and cares about you, sort of like Bill Clinton (except Junior doesn't face-fuck fat girls; he prefers broken porn stars). Junior has this way of making you want to be around him and love him, and Morimoto was no different. So after a while, I planned a trip up to see Junior and of course get to meet one of my few living heroes.

Morimoto has a place in NYC, and he and Junior were going to be there for a week or so doing some stuff, so Junior invited me up to come hang with them. I wasn't as excited as I was when I went to the midget convention in Milwaukee, but I was about as fucking psyched as I could be to meet another man.

Junior "Here's the thing though, man: Be cool. Morimoto doesn't like most people. He's very much a traditional Japanese chef in his approach to life and people."
Tucker "I don't like most people either. It's perfect."
Junior "But you know how hierarchical and rigid they can be in some things?"
Tucker "Dude, in my boarding school, I coached dozens of F.O.B. Asians through chemistry and biology. I can handle this, no problem."

We all met for lunch at some fancy hot new NYC restaurant, and since the Iron Chef was with us we got the prime table, right next to this huge koi pond in the middle of the restaurant.

The first thing you notice about Morimoto is that he speaks two languages, neither of which is English. He speaks Japanese and what I call "Morimoto." Junior had to translate from "Morimoto English" to standard English for me at first, but I quickly got the hang of it.

Second, Morimoto was pretty much exactly like I thought he'd be: quiet, professional, reserved. No problem, I can play it cool too. I had just read *Shogun,* so I actually knew some Japanese and I used those words correctly at various conversational points. And every time I addressed Morimoto, I called him "Chef." This is actually a big deal in Japan. In America, kitchens are places where talented but undisciplined people go to work and snort coke. It's the opposite in Japan. Being a chef there is one of the most respected jobs—akin to being a doctor in America—and they get treated with an immense amount of respect. Food and cooking also have something of a spiritual importance to the Japanese, and the kitchen is a place of reverence and discipline.

For example, at one point, the waiter took Morimoto's finished plate away, and took chopsticks off and put them back on the table, with one end on the little rock that fancy places have. But he wasn't paying attention and put the chopsticks down with the food-touching end on the table. Morimoto noticed immediately, and reproached him.

Morimoto "No. Chopstick go other way. Otherwise, rock have no meaning."

And then of course, once we started talking about food, it was on. And when Junior mentioned to Morimoto that I was an "Iron Chef" fan, and I started talking about the Battle Porcini episode where he made the mushroom crème brûlée, he realized I was not just some idiot; I actually had an idea of what I was talking about. Like any true artist, he loved talking about the complexities and artistry of what he did, and we must have gone over every dish in that episode.

The conversation was great, but sadly the restaurant was not. It was clearly one of those places for people who think they're better'n me. Which is fine, if the food and service really are that good. Except they weren't. After the entree plates sat finished in front of us for about 20 minutes, I joked we should throw the chicken bones in the koi pond to feed the fish. Morimoto thought that was fucking hilarious. We busted on the restaurant for a while more, and then after lunch went our separate ways. Junior called me a few hours later.

Junior "That went great. I've never seen him actually warm to someone that quickly. He likes you a lot."

Tucker "That's cool, I really like him a lot too. He's a cool guy."

Junior "He said he would definitely hang out with you again."

Tucker "You do realize we're talking about how much a Japanese guy is into me, right? This is weird. I'm going."

And yes, if you were inclined to make some sort of gay/bromance/man date joke, this would be the appropriate place. Those of you inclined to do that can go fuck yourselves.

We went out drinking/eating a few more times together. There aren't really many funny stories to tell; it was just guys hanging out, breaking each other's balls and having fun. There was one incident, though, that was noteworthy:

One night out we all got really bombed, and like a fucking idiot, I got my car towed. Once I figured out where the NYC Tow Pound was and how to get my car back, it was already 2am, so I told Junior and Morimoto I'd see them later. Except Morimoto wanted to come with me.

Morimoto "I live New York City twenty years, many cars get towed, never see tow pound. I come. We go."

I have done a lot of really weird shit in my life, but walking into the NYC Tow Pound with Iron Chef Morimoto, and watching one of the DMV ladies scream and come out for a picture is at the top.

And of course, I couldn't help but snap a pic too [that's me, Morimoto, and Junior]:

Fast forward to a few months later:

This was 2005, back before the Green Zone in Iraq was just a normal US military base, and soldiers needed pretty basic stuff like toilet paper and shit. Since I have so many friends and fans in the military, my buddies and I stateside organized a series of parties called "Tanked for the Troops" where we'd do some bar event to raise money, then use the money to buy sundries and supplies for soldiers in Iraq, and ship it to them. Pretty basic, but it was a ton of fun, and there was no bullshit involved. Most charities are 30% or more overhead. We took every dollar we got (and more) and used it for stuff that helped real people who really needed it. That's what charity should be.

Anyway, I scheduled a Tanked for the Troops event in NYC, and invited Morimoto to co-host it with me. Morimoto agreed. This turned it from a rinky-dink little thing my buddies and I were doing, to something that was a much bigger deal. We amped up promotion and billed it as something where Morimoto and I would do like an Iron-Chef-style competition, but with shots. It didn't work out that way for two reasons:

1. I know food, but I am not even qualified to be one of his assistants on "Iron Chef"—those guys are all amazing and accomplished chefs in their own right— much less actually COMPETE with him.

2. Sadly, the bar we booked it at was a complete clusterfuck. I am not even going to name the bar and give them any press, fuck them. But basically, they had nothing ready and were totally unprepared.

Thankfully, Junior and I are resourceful motherfuckers. We pulled together a ton of random items and Morimoto and I went behind the bar with the other four regular bartenders working alongside us to get drinks and shit for everyone else in the place. Then, instead of competing with him, I became Morimoto's de facto assistant, like on "Iron Chef." Someone at the bar would pick an item from the things Junior and I had collected earlier, like tortilla chips, and give it to Morimoto. I would gather up all the other things Morimoto asked for and then, using that patron-selected ingredient, Morimoto would make up a tasty shot. He not only did it, he made up fantastic shots for EACH of the things below:

 Tortilla chips
 Tabasco
 Salt
 Pepper
 Maraschino Cherries
 Whiskey
 Lemon
 Olives

It was kind of amazing what he could do with these things, and I wish I had either recorded it all or written it down, because some of the shots were good enough I'd want to have them again. Sadly, I was too busy getting hammered—remember, we DID the shot for each one of those theme ingredients.

Despite all the problems, it was a great time. Even normally standoffish Morimoto was drunk and happy. As we walked out from behind the bar, he pulled me aside:

Morimoto "This . . . very fun. I do event with you . . . anytime."
Tucker "Thank you chef, I had a great time too."

By then, the bar was totally packed. I was talking to the two girls who'd come out to fuck me, and everyone else was getting pictures with Morimoto or just having a good time. Not paying attention to anything, about maybe 45 minutes pass, and some people convince Morimoto to get back behind the bar and make another exotic Iron Chef shot. Neither Junior nor I noticed this as it was happening, otherwise one of us would have gone with him to be his assistant, because the idiot bartenders weren't going to do it.

I didn't see what happened next, but my buddy was right there and saw the whole thing go down. He said that Morimoto was a little drunk, and I guess just assumed that the normal bartenders would assist him the same way that I had before. He's fucking Iron Chef Morimoto, why wouldn't they, right? So he'd need Jack Daniels, and yell out for Jack Daniels, and these meathead guido bartenders would just look at him like he was an idiot and go about their business. This frustrated Morimoto obviously, and at some point, one of the bartenders bumped into him. My buddy says he thinks it may not have been intentional, but the dude basically hip-checked Morimoto into the bar sink. This is about when I turned around and saw the commotion.

This did not sit well with Morimoto. He turned around and got in the dude's face and yelled something in Japanese at him. The bartender did the only thing a meathead guido can do: he got violent and pushed Morimoto. Well, Morimoto went straight-up Billy Martin on the bartender, and chest-bumped him back so hard the bartender fell back against the back of the bar. Three of the other bartenders tried to grab Morimoto, but he pushed them off of him, and then grabbed three pint glasses and threw them down on the ground so hard they shattered on the floor. The four bartenders then converged on Morimoto, like in a cartoon.

At that point, Junior saw what was going on and did a full-on leap OVER the bar like he was Mitch Fucking Gaylord or something, took out two of the bartenders, and got up swinging. He went fucking nuts; I think he may have knocked one bartender out cold. It was like *Tango & Cash* meets *Cocktail.* My buddy and I ran to help. We pulled one bartender out, but by that point the bouncers had come over, and the Action Jackson bar fight had dissolved into a scrum of limbs and pushing. The next thing I know, me, Junior, and Morimoto are out on the street.

It took a second to process . . . but then it dawned on me: I just got thrown out of a charity event.

No—I JUST GOT KICKED OUT OF **MY OWN** CHARITY EVENT!!!!

How does this happen? I didn't even know that was possible. Who has ever done that? Who has ever been kicked out of their own charity event?

Tucker Max, that's who.

About a year later, I was hanging out with Morimoto and Junior again, and that incident came up:

Morimoto "That . . . pretty funny."
Tucker "Yeah, it was pretty funny."
Morimoto "Your writing . . . now, I understand."

JUNIOR'S MARRIAGE

Occurred, December 2001

And then there's this story. As you read this, you're going to think, "this can't be real." You're going to think that there is no fucking way this could happen. I agree. Had I not been there when he got back to my place, seen the evidence on his sweater, and then seen the article in the paper a few days later, I'd have trouble believing this too. But what can I say? Real life is stranger than fiction.

When I moved to Boca Raton after law school, I lived in Mizner Park, right above my dad's restaurant. I had a two-bedroom apartment, and coincidentally, Junior was looking for a place to live. Perfect situation: I get to live with my best friend; he gets a nice place that he couldn't get otherwise because his credit is worse than Lenny Dykstra's.

Nothing comes without a price, not even living in a sweet apartment with your best friend. As we were figuring out the apartment details, we had this conversation:

Junior "OK, but just so you know my girlfriend is going to be spending a lot of time over here."
Tucker "Well, you're dating her, I'd expect that I guess."
Junior "I mean . . . a LOT of time."
Tucker "Motherfucker—do not fuck with me. You know I will set that bitch on fire and throw her off the balcony."
Junior "Dude . . . she is my girlfriend."
Tucker "You know me . . ."
Junior "I'm dating her . . ."
Tucker "Bitches ain't shit!"
Junior "Well . . . we're engaged."

Tucker "Why . . . when . . . what is wrong with you?? You fucking asshole. The only way I'd let her live here is if you are paying DOUBLE rent."
Junior "Done!"
Tucker "FUCK!"

Let me explain. At the time, Junior was dating/engaged to a woman named DemonWhore. Her name was not actually DemonWhore, that's just what it should have been if her parents had been responsible citizens. In my humble opinion, DemonWhore was the most vile she-devil cunt in the history of women. I fucking HATED everything about this bitch. You may think I'm being harsh. You are wrong. Imagine the worst woman you've ever known; DemonWhore is worse. I could go on and on about what a horrible piece of shit DemonWhore was. A perfect example of the type of person she is: DemonWhore was like 39 at the time (Junior was 26, I think) and had a 19 year old daughter who was a homeless crack addict, literally sucking dick on the street for rock. And DemonWhore is such a horrifically selfish human being that she refused to help her out in any way. DemonWhore is probably the most classic case of Borderline Personality Disorder I've ever actually met in person. [BPD is what Hitler and Stalin had. Basically pure evil.]

[And yes, the next question is what does it say about my friend that he was dating her? Believe me, I ask him about this all the time now. He doesn't want to think about it.]

So they move in, and because DemonWhore knows I hate her fucking guts, she is on her best behavior around me. She also makes sure to keep basically everything they do a secret from me. It wasn't hard: she had Junior so fucking wrapped, it was ridiculous. The extent of their secret life was so complete that they got married while they lived with me, and I didn't know. Not kidding at all.

One night they are out to dinner alone, kinda drunk, and they decide they want to get married. Not eventually. THAT NIGHT. Well, because DemonWhore is a whore who has fucked most of the rich and powerful men in Boca, she called up two friends of hers: A priest who could marry them, and a lawyer to witness it.

Since this was the very definition of last minute, they couldn't set up anything special or do it anywhere appropriate. So they decided to get married in the next best place: a public park. Like where homeless people shit and old people wait for death. I'm not joking one bit.

At the end of Palmetto Park Road in Boca Raton is a park called South Beach Park. Palmetto Park Road is a major thoroughfare, but it dead-ends into the parking lot for that park. At the far end of the parking lot is a public gazebo that overlooks the ocean. It's a pretty cool place, and people go there all the time to have picnics or drink and hang out or whatever. Or sometimes get married.

They told the priest and the witness to meet them there. It was about 11:00 at night, and when they got there, there were some teenagers sitting in the gazebo, smoking some swag weed and drinking warm beers they stole from the convenience store. Junior could sell gag reflex to a hooker, so he has no problem convincing these kids to leave . . . so he can get married.

The priest and the witness show up, and they get started on their marriage ceremony. The wedding is being held in a gazebo, in a public park. With discarded Natty Light cans and stubbed-out roaches still strewn about.

Anyway, they are exchanging their vows, and they get to the part where the priest is talking bullshit about the ring symbolizing some nonsense . . . when they hear a loud tire squeal out on Palmetto Park Road, and then an engine revving. They look out to the street, and about half a mile away is a BMW 3 Series, quickly accelerating down the street right towards them. BMWs can fucking move, and this thing had the pedal to the floor.

It caromed down Palmetto Park, bouncing off a few cars before straightening out, headed straight towards the gazebo where Junior and Demon-Whore were drunkenly and surreptitiously tying the knot.

The car wasn't slowing down . . . 20 . . . 25 . . . 30 . . . 35 . . . 40 . . . 45 . . .

It was probably going well over 50 miles an hour when it crossed A1A and slammed directly into the sea wall, not 20 feet from the gazebo. The front of the car crumpled, twisted metal and glass flew everywhere, and the airbags exploded in the two passengers' faces. The incredible noise of crashing car was immediately followed by the horn going off and getting stuck.

After the initial shock, the four of them ran over to the car. If you've never seen a fresh accident scene, it's hard to describe. You really should google "car accident pictures" and look at some to get an idea of what they encountered—it was that grisly.

The person in the driver's seat was male. His face was a mess of contusions and trauma. He wasn't dead, but he was really fucked up. The woman in the passenger seat was fucked up as well, groaning, bleeding everywhere, but not as bad.

Junior pulls the woman out of the car as DemonWhore calls 911. He holds her in his arms, and she starts blabbing incoherently. Eventually Junior starts to make out clipped phrases like . . .

"No, please . . . I'm so sorry . . . no, don't do this . . . it was a mistake . . . no, please . . . he tried to kill us . . ."

Eventually the cops and paramedics show up to deal with the scene. The EMTs started working on the woman right away, but had to wait for the fire department to cut the guy out of the driver's side with the Jaws of Life. By the time they got him out of the car, he was in critical condition. They gave him CPR as they loaded him into the ambulance and took him to the hospital. The cop wasn't sure if she was going to make it or not, either.

The cops interviewed Junior, DemonWhore, and their two witnesses, and got statements from all of them. The cop at the scene tells Junior that he isn't sure, but he would guess that this is a domestic case, and that they are going to treat it like an attempted murder-suicide until they get more evidence. So basically, at this moment at least, it appears that a couple was in such a horrific and fucked up fight that the man tried to kill them both with his car. At Junior's wedding.

By the time this is all done and the cops tell them they can leave, it is probably 1am. You can imagine the mental state of the wedding party at that point. Everyone is worked up and emotionally exhausted—they just witnessed a traumatic car wreck that was a potential murder-suicide. Junior has the woman's blood on his sweater. Everyone of course assumes that the wedding is over.

Junior "OK, thanks for coming out guys. We'll try this again next weekend."
DemonWhore "I bet the Deerfield Beach pier will be empty right now."
Junior "What? Deerfield? DemonWhore, I'm not getting married right now."

She starts getting hysterical.

DemonWhore "If we don't do it now, it'll never happen!"

Junior looked at her like she'd just punched a baby.

Junior "You can't be serious."
DemonWhore "Well, we wanted to get married tonight!"
Junior "ARE YOU OUT OF YOUR MIND!!!! WERE YOU HERE FOR THE CAR WRECK??"
DemonWhore "I KNEW YOU WEREN'T GOING TO MARRY ME!"
Junior "I STILL HAVE BLOOD ON MY SWEATER!!"

This went on for at least ten minutes. DemonWhore threw such a fit, bitched and complained so much . . . Junior relented. They went to the Deerfield Beach pier, and got married. With the blood of a relationship that was so bad, someone tried to end it by driving a car into a seawall, still on the sweater of the groom. GOT MARRIED WITH BLOOD STILL ON HIS SWEATER.

SLOPPY SECONDS

Here's the best part: Junior and DemonWhore came home that night and told me the whole story. Where they were, what the car looked like, I even saw the blood on his sweater. They just left out one small little detail . . . THE ENTIRE PART ABOUT A WEDDING. I knew something was weird to begin with—I couldn't figure out why the fuck they would be in the Palmetto Park gazebo that late at night—but it never would have occurred to me in a million years that they were there to get MARRIED. It made no sense.

Maybe six months later, Junior moved out and told me the news: He and DemonWhore had gotten married. Not really a shock, except I was kinda pissed he didn't even invite me to the wedding.

Junior "Well, it was kind of an impromptu thing. There was only me, her, a priest and a lawyer."
Tucker "When was this?"
Junior "Well . . . that's the other thing . . ."

He filled in the blanks. I almost shit myself.

While Junior is religious in the normal way that most people are, I am not. I don't practice any sort of religion and I don't believe in God, at least not in the type of God that organized monotheistic religions are based on. And I don't really even believe in fate, at least not in the way most people think of fate, but still . . . sometimes certain signs should not be ignored.

Tucker "Junior, YOU BELIEVE IN GOD!! If there was EVER a time to believe in that type of shit, if there was EVER a time to pay attention to the signs that the universe sends you, THIS WAS THE FUCKING TIME!"
Junior "Yeah."
Tucker "God was so against you marrying her, he TRIED TO KILL A COUPLE AT YOUR WEDDING!!"
Junior "I know."
Tucker "AND YOU STILL GOT MARRIED!!???!?!!?! THAT VERY NIGHT!!!"
Junior "Yeah."

Tucker "WITH THE BLOOD OF THE WOMAN ON YOUR SWEATER!!!!"

Junior "Yeah."

Tucker "Oh my lord. DemonWhore is so much more evil than I realized. Dude . . . don't bother praying anymore. God is done with you. The only person in history to get a clearer message from God was Moses. After ignoring this sign, even an all-forgiving God would forsake you."

Want to predict what happened?

Thank God it was just divorce. Thank GOD they didn't have kids. The actual divorce was just as disastrous as any awful divorce you've heard of. I am pretty sure DemonWhore's first settlement request even demanded a share in Junior's soul. This basically sums her up: The divorce court judge, after dealing with DemonWhore for a month in multiple motions and hearings, got so fed up, he said this to DemonWhore—FROM THE BENCH:

Judge "You are the most evil, sadistic wench who has ever come before my court, and I've been doing divorces in south Florida for almost 15 years."

Direct, verbatim quote. When you are so awful you get a DIVORCE COURT judge in SOUTH FLORIDA to say that to you . . . you're the absolute worst of the worst. And yet, Junior still married her.

Boca Raton/Delray Beach News - Monday, December 31, 2001 5

Smashed wall at pavilion to be fixed

Car crash that injured two knocks down section of barrier

Police may file charges against driver who crashed into the seawall

Wall / from 5

will be advertised for bids in February. The unanticipated wall repair will be rolled into that work.

Scott said the reconstruction is expected to begin in May.

In the meantime, Boca Raton Police are considering filing charges against the driver of a 1999 BMW that was traveling an estimated 45 to 50 miles per hour when it crashed into the seawall, according to a police report.

The driver, identified by police as Haydir Mohsin Al-Hasnawi, 31, of North Lauderdale, told investigators he was driving his girlfriend's car east on East Palmetto Park Road approaching Ocean Boulevard just after 8:30 p.m. That's when a white car pulled out from a side street or parking lot into his path, the report said.

According to police, Al-Haswani tried to apply the brake but instead stepped on the accelerator. Police said the car sped up the semi-circular parking lot leading to the pavilion, knocked down a "No Parking" sign, snapped off a palm tree and then struck the wall.

Boca Raton Fire-Rescue took both Al-Hasnawi and his girlfriend, Karen Bernadette Yee, 33, of Pembroke Pines, to Delray Medical Center. She was treated and released, police said.

The driver was held for a day and then released.

Police said the accident caused an estimated $20,000 damage to the seawall.

Yee told police the couple was returning to a hotel in Deerfield Beach when the accident occurred.

Where is Junior Now

Junior is still one of my best friends on earth, but has his shit together much more than he used to. He now owns restaurants in Florida, and though still dates broken, fucked up women, *nothing* as bad as Demon-Whore. I don't even think that's possible.

I go visit him all the time in the West Palm Beach area. If you follow me on Twitter (@tuckermax), I usually tweet about when I go to his restaurants, so you can come meet him. Unlike most of my friends, he likes it when people know him from my books.

Some glimpses into my childhood

People are always asking me about what I was like as a kid growing up or in high school or shit like that. I don't fucking know. I never write about those periods in my life because I'm not a fucking biographer and I don't particularly enjoy chronicling trauma survival—I like writing funny, engaging and entertaining stories about my life, not annoying little anecdotes about shitty aspects of my childhood.

That being said, I do have a few childhood stories that are kinda funny:

MOM!

When I was a kid, my mother was a flight attendant. As a result, I spent many hours of my childhood riding on planes. I'd probably been to 15 countries by the time I was 5.

One time, when I was about 3 or 4, my mother and I were flying somewhere. She wasn't working this flight, so we were travelling as passengers in normal passenger seats. I was sitting on her lap, because I was still at the age (and size) where it was cute and convenient (and legal) to do that. About midway through the flight, I had to take a shit.

Even at this young age I thought I was king of the world, completely independent, and could do anything I wanted. I had just learned how to use the bathroom myself, so flush with my newfound potty training skills,

I told my mom I could go make a poop without her help. I walked down the aisle, opened the door, turned and pulled the latch back like I'd been taught, and got on the throne.

I was right: I was more than capable of taking a shit without any help from anyone. But when I was finished, I realized that I couldn't quite perform all of the essential functions of bathroom duty, so I opened the door, and yelled down the plane:

"MOM! COME WIPE MY BUTT!"

A smattering of nervous laughter broke out across the plane as my poor, horribly embarrassed mother got up from her seat in the front of the plane, and walked all the way to the back to tend to my request.

I JUST LIKE TO SAY 'SMOCK'

My mom and I had a lot of arguments in my youth. Most weren't that funny, at least not to me, but one that does make me laugh is the argument that led me to discover that I unequivocally was smarter than her.

For most of my early life, I thought I might be smarter than my mom. Until I got to be about 10 or 11, that was probably just childhood hubris. Around 12 though, I started to realize I might be right. I remembered things better, I did calculations in my head faster, I always seemed a step ahead of her. This is not to say I thought my mom was a dumbass—I was just a genius, and I developed pretty quickly intellectually.

My mom loved Scrabble, and I would play with her a lot and she would always beat me. Until the day of this story. I was stomping her all over the board, ahead by at least 50 points with maybe five words left apiece. She put some word on that went to the edge of the board, and I struck gold on my next turn, triple word scoring with "smock" to further extend my lead.

She had completely crap letters, and could not find anything decent. She would normally throw them in and skip the turn, but being so far behind she had to get some points with what she had. As a last ditch effort, she added an "O" to the "K" at the end of "smock" forming "OK." No chance. I called her out for violating the Scrabble rule that prohibited abbreviations.

We argued for like 20 minutes. And not the good kind of argument where she makes legit linguistic points and I refute them—this thing was ad hominem all the way, with both of us cursing and insulting each other. It was like a scene straight out of "Intervention".

Finally, I had enough, grabbed the dictionary, found "OK", pointed at the 'abbrv' sign right next to it and shoved it right in front of her fucking face to see. She blurted out an angry:

Mom "I DON'T CARE WHAT THAT DAMN THING SAYS, IT'S A WORD TO ME!"
Tucker "YOU'RE FUCKING WRONG AND I'M SMARTER THAN YOU!"
Mom "I AM YOUR MOTHER AND I AM KEEPING MY POINTS!"

I took the dictionary and smashed it on the Scrabble board, then turned over the whole table on top of her, scattering the tiles everywhere.

That was the last time we ever played Scrabble.

GUACAMOLE IS DELICIOUS

My dad grew up around the food business and still owns restaurants to this day (Max's Grille in Boca Raton is the flagship). As a result, I've been exposed to a lot of food experiences, especially at an early age. I can remember trying things like caviar, lobster, sea urchin, veal, and any number of other unusual or exotic foods, and of course, most were extremely delicious.

One time, I was about 11 years old, I was in Florida visiting my dad and step-mom, and her parents—my step-grandparents—were there as well. The five of us were at dinner, and being that it was fall and soft-shell crab season—one of my favorite foods—I ordered the special.

The dish came out and looked fantastic. It had an Asian fusion theme and soy sauce with it, but whatever—it was pan-seared soft-shell crab. You could garish it with cat poop and it'd still be awesome. Next to the ramekin of soy sauce, I noticed these big, almond shaped green things.

Tucker "Dad, what's this?"

Without the slightest hesitation my Dad responds:

Dad "That's a special type of guacamole."
Tucker "Guacamole is delicious!"
Dad "That's especially good, pop it in your mouth and try it."

I grab it, shove it in my mouth and start happily chewing on it. There is no obvious flavor at first . . .

. . . then all of the sudden, my mouth EXPLODES from the heat, my nostrils are seared by violent pain, my throat feels like it's being gripped in a vice . . .

. . . and I vomit all over the table. All over everyone's food, plates, everything.

It wasn't guacamole at all. It was a full slab of wasabi (Japanese horse-radish). That I ate all at once, vigorously chewing, not having any idea what I was in for.

StepMom "Oh my God Dennis, look what he did!"

My dad and step-grandfather almost die they are laughing so hard. I mean that literally—my step-grandfather choked on his food and almost had to have the Heimlich applied he was laughing so hard, and my dad nearly blew a vein in his forehead from laughter.

I was not laughing. It took me at least three hours, and gallons of water, to get the wasabi taste out of my mouth, nose and lungs. For a fucking food guy, my dad could have at least told me that water only makes it worse and you need to drink milk to mute the pain. Maybe if he hadn't been laughing so hard, he would have thought to tell me.

HOW I LEARNED TO MASTURBATE

There are only two types of liars: Those that say they don't, and those that say they quit. Everyone masturbates. The only people who don't masturbate are eunuchs and midgets whose arms are too short to reach their privates.

I'm no different. I love jacking off. At this point in my life, I still masturbate at least once a day, and that's even if I'm having regular sex with a girl(s). I used to be way worse—when I was 22, if I found a good video on the internet, I'd skip a class to rub a few out.

If you are too young, stupid, or repressed to have found your genitals yet, you may be asking yourself why I've incorporated masturbation into my daily schedule with such fierce dedication. The positives are numerous: you know your body better than anyone else, it's quick, free, easy, and fun. And these positives far outweigh the negatives, which are none.

Masturbation is not better than having sex with a girl, but it can definitely be better than dealing with all the girl's shit. There have been dozens of girls in my lifetime who, when presented with the chance to fuck them, I've turned them down and masturbated instead, simply because I knew that after I shot my nut, my hand would not get pregnant, not give me an STD, and not expect me to entertain it or stay awake talking about shit I don't care about.

As much as I love masturbation, I started doing it late in life. Because I grew up in Kentucky in the early 90's, before the internet really existed in a meaningful way, I wasn't even fully sure what masturbation was until I got to be like 13 or 14. I just knew it was supposedly awful and anyone suspected of it was summarily mocked, so I never really thought much about it.

Don't get me wrong; I had plenty of my uncle's old porn stashed under my bed, I just thought you were supposed to look at it, like a study guide or a topographical map. What if a girl you were with decided to do yoga on a pool table and rest her shoulders on the felt in downward dog position while she tucked her head underneath her leg, sucked on her tit, stuck her ass up in the air and pressed the tip of a pool cue against her clit (my uncle liked *Hustler*)? You needed to be prepared.

I had no idea porn had another purpose. I didn't even think it was weird at all that when I lost my virginity on my 16th birthday, I had NEVER masturbated. It wasn't until more than a year later, when I was 17, that I popped my hand cherry. And that happened just by chance.

I was hanging out with a girl in my basement who evidently had one of those dads who loved her and paid attention to her, because she wouldn't sleep with me or give head. Fucking great. Now what? She started to rub her hand up and down my cock. I liked it a lot, and then—to my mild shock—I came all over her. She was not pleased. The best part was that this only pissed her off because she "had just washed that shirt." Ah, Kentucky.

So the next day I call her to come over but she is busy or whatever. Then it dawns on me: that thing she did, with her hand . . . I could do that myself. I have hands. I can rub one up and down too. So I try it.

It worked! And in quite the revelation, I discover that I am even better at it than she was. I'm a fucking natural!

So I do it again.

And lo and behold, it works again! Just as good as the last time! This whole masturbation thing is fucking great. Why has everyone been so down on it?

I go again. And then one more time. You know, for luck.

Later that night, I pulled out one of my uncle's *Hustler* magazines. It was like looking at it for the first time all over again. That's when I realized: porn isn't a study guide. It's a masturbatory aid! By the time I was done, I was exhausted, and that magazine looked like someone had dropped it in a swimming pool.

The well-adjusted girl with appropriate sexual boundaries called me the next day:

Girl "Hey, can I come over?"
Tucker "Do you want to have sex?"
Girl "No—I told you, I don't want to have sex until college."
Tucker "Will you go down on me?"
Girl "No, I don't like that. But we can, you know, do the other thing. But you need to be more careful this time, like where it goes."
Tucker "Nah, just forget it. I've . . . found someone better."

Ambi-jerk-strous

About three months after I learned how to jack off, a catastrophe happened: I tore my rotator cuff, and had to have my right arm immobilized and in a sling for three months.

Granted, this effectively ended any hopes that my baseball career would extend past high school. I played catcher and had a really good arm*, but since I couldn't hit a fucking breaking ball to save my life, I wasn't really banking on the athletic route anyway. No, this was such a disaster because it meant I couldn't use my right arm for anything for three months.

ANYTHING.

I lasted about a week without jacking off before I was ready to go insane. Literally insane. I had to get these stored up loads out of me. I took the sling off and tried to jack it anyway. I would have fought through the intense pain if I had been able to cum, but sadly, stabbing, searing, tearing pain in your shoulder inhibits erections.

I didn't know what to do, I really didn't. I didn't have a girlfriend at the time, I was still only 17, and not good enough with women yet that I had a stable of booty calls in the wings. It was up to me, and I was going crazy. Then it hit me:

I HAVE TWO HANDS!!! What about my left?

I distinctly remember looking down at my left, like it wasn't part of my body, and wondering if he was really ready to come off the bench, without warming up, and take the game winning shot.

But without other options, I put him in. It was different, rocky and rough at times, but effective. With some more reps, he actually started to do a good job.

I became officially ambi-jerk-strous.

Leftie eventually became like Lou Gehrig—once he got in, he never went out. I pinch-hit with my right every now and then, but 90% of the time, I stay with my starter.

And that is why, even to this day, I masturbate with my left hand, even though I'm right handed. You can even see the difference in my physiology: My left forearm is slightly bigger than my right.

Footnotes

*Here's an example of how good my arm was at 15:

This one kid would always take big leads off second, then walk back after the pitch with his head down. I knew if I came up throwing I wouldn't get him; he'd either be tipped off by the coaches yelling or the second base-man running to cover the bag. I had a good arm, but not good enough to get him if he was trying to get back. I had to figure out another way to get him.

When he got a lead off double, I called a conference at the mound, and told the second baseman to wait until the pitch crossed the plate, then just casually walk over to the bag, that the throw was coming down, but to act like it wasn't. I told the pitcher to put the ball well outside, and that on the return throw, to act like he was going to catch it, but let it go through to the second baseman.

He put the pitch way off the plate, and I kinda slid a bit for the ball, staying on my knees and pausing after I caught it, showing the ball in my hand to the runner. The kid took an extra step towards third, saw I had the ball, and, because I stayed on my knees, he put his head down and just started casually walking back towards second. Staying on my knees, I slowly pulled the ball back like I was just going to throw it to pitcher, then at the last second, whipped it as hard as I could, still from my knees, towards second base. The pitcher played it perfectly, putting his glove up two feet away from the ball, but still acting like he was going to catch it. The second baseman was only a few feet off the bag by now, and was perfectly nonchalant, pretending like nothing was happening. The runner was so confused when the ball snapped into the second baseman's glove and he got tagged out.

When people realized what had happened, the crowd (just parents and girlfriends, mainly) erupted. I had picked off a base runner, from my knees, at second base. The home plate ump actually had to explain to

---

the opposing coach what happened; he'd missed my throw and didn't believe it at first.

I immediately became a legend; not one single person attempted to steal a base on me the rest of the season. Coaches would scream at their players if they took even a two-step lead on me, on any base. Everyone ignored all the tricks I had to pull to pick the guy off, they just knew I picked a dude off at second from my knees, so ipso facto, I must have the greatest arm in the history of Babe Ruth catchers.

And yes, you are correct: I am grown man and just wrote a 500-word footnote about a completely meaningless athletic feat I accomplished almost 20 years ago, in a teenager's baseball league.

Yeah, well fuck you. You write multiple best sellers that create a new literary genre, sell millions of copies, and inspire a movie—all before you're 35—and you can earn the privilege to obnoxiously indulge yourself about whatever you want as well.

THE MARLEY STORIES

Occurred, October 2002

When I first moved to Chicago in 2002 to write full time, I lived with a friend of mine, TheRoommate. His brother went on a long vacation and didn't want to board his dog, so he left him with us for a month. He was a 5-year-old yellow lab named "Marley" (they named him before that awful book *Marley and Me* came out) and these are all the funny things that happened when I was taking care of him.

[As you read these, please remember that I'd never had a dog of my own up to that point, so a lot of what I did reflects a complete lack of knowledge on how to deal with dogs. In 2005 I got my current dog, Murph, and learned everything I didn't know then. So please don't tell me I was walking Marley the wrong way or rewarding negative behavior or something. I know. It's been fixed, Cesar Milan. So mind your own fucking business.]

DOGGY BASICS

The very first day Marley shows up, I get very excited and want to take him for a walk to try to meet some girls. As I head out the door, my roommate's brother hands me a plastic bag.

Tucker "What the fuck is this for?"
Jason "It's not all about picking up girls; you have to pick up other things too when you have a dog."
Tucker "WHAT! I have to pick up the dog's shit? Are you kidding? This is not happening."

Jason "No, dude, you really have to do it. It's the law."
Tucker "Fine."

I take the bag, and tell Marley:

Tucker "If you ever shit when I am walking you, I'm going to make you eat it. You're only allowed to poop when TheRoommate walks you."

He licks all over my face with the same tongue he uses to lick other dogs' asses and his little doggy penis. Great, we haven't even cuddled yet and the dog's already gone ass-to-mouth on me. Thanks, buddy.

Not even ten minutes into the walk, my plan works and Marley and I run into two girls sitting outside a bar. They see Marley and start with the "Awww, wook at da wittle puppy!" babytalk that tells you these girls have maternal instincts and are ready to tend to your every need. Like me, Marley is a big fan of attractive young ladies, so he runs up to them and starts licking one all over her face.

Tucker "Marley! Don't do that—you don't know where her face has been."

She was not as amused about this as she should have been. That line was gold.

WHY RESPONSIBILITY CAN SUCK

I left my apartment at 6pm and went to an "All You Can Drink." Bar specials like this are paradoxes to me. They are both "A Reason To Live," and "A Potential Way To Die."

I remember very little about the night. Including, apparently, some girl I introduced myself to who responded with, "You don't remember me, do you?" If that happens, your best bet is to just walk away. Nothing you can say will save the situation, even if you offer to hook up with her again to refresh your memory.

I stumbled back to my place around 3am, and was abruptly woken at 6am by a girl enthusiastically licking my face. I grabbed her head to guide her mouth to a more appropriate place for her tongue, but she just wriggled a lot and started playfully biting my hands. What the fuck? I wondered if I brought home a Northwestern softball player. Her furry, floppy ears added to my confusion. Finally, my hung over brain realized that the girl in my bed was not a girl at all, but Marley the dog. I was way too tired to get up and walk him, so I pushed him off and passed back out.

Did you know that dogs need to use the bathroom at regular intervals, just like humans? And that these needs exist completely independent of you, and are not at all considerate of how hung over you are?

Yes, well, I knew this at the time, I just didn't really think about the implications of making Marley hold it for 18 hours. Namely, he can't. When I finally woke up around 1pm, he had a nice surprise for me.

OK, that's fine, when you have to go, you have to go, right? But he took it a step farther. Not content with just relieving himself, Marley decided to make a statement, to let me know just how pissed he was.

He urinated directly on my laundry pile, creating a nice big yellow stain all over my dirty clothes. Thanks Marley, I get the message. If you're not gonna go out, neither am I.

MARLEY GOES TO DOG PARK, HUMPS EVERYTHING

There is a dog park called "Wiggly Field" about ten blocks from my house. There are always good looking girls there with their dogs, so of course, I take Marley as much as possible.

We show up the first time, I let him loose, and start a conversation with a nice looking woman. Apparently, Marley thought I had taken him to a Roman bathhouse, because he started running around aggressively humping every dog that would stand still for two seconds. Which led to a conversation that I could never have imagined myself having with another human being:

Tucker "Gosh, I'm really sorry that my dog keeps humping your dog."
Dog owner "Oh, it's OK. She's fixed."
Tucker "Yeah, so is he, but it doesn't seem to stop him, which really confuses me. I'm trying to figure out where he gets all this testosterone. Maybe he was hanging out with Sammy Sosa, I don't know."

Chatting up a beautiful young lady isn't easy when she's trying to keep an eye on her sweet little puppy dog. It's even harder when you have to continually stop your dog from raping her dog because he's hornier than R. Kelly in an elementary school.

Marley does this every time we go now. The worst part is, he humps indiscriminately. Young or old, big or small, male or female—he doesn't care. He's like the Ricky Martin of dogs. They're all pink on the inside to him.

Yes, there is gorgeous symbolism in this, and yes, it is perfect poetic justice that my dog does this, blah, blah, blah—shut the fuck up. All I want is to be able to talk to that cute girl with the collie without Marley humping her dog like he's going to the electric chair.

MARLEY GOES TO BAR, FINALLY EARNS HIS KEEP

I'm not sure there is a better way to pick up women, save being famous, than by owning a dog and taking it to a bar. I don't know if you've ever taken a dog into a bar, but if you haven't, then put it at the top of your

"To-Do" list. There is a bar right by my place in Chicago that allows dogs and the first time I took him with me it was like shooting skanks in a barrel. I should have figured. Marley is a super cute and friendly yellow lab; obviously they all want to pet the doggy. Every girl who saw him would come up to pet him—of course he loved the attention—and he'd welcome her by wagging his tail and licking her face and smelling her crotch. If only it were so simple.

One girl in particular adored Marley. Wanted to do nothing but pet him. She was possibly the most needy girl I've ever met in my life. Within the first five minutes of talking to her I knew she wanted a boyfriend, she couldn't meet guys, she had so much love to give, etc., etc. Judging by her reaction to Marley's non-stop sloppy kisses, this was the most action she'd gotten in quite awhile. She was virtually making out with him.

I quickly got sick of her using me (and Marley) as a metaphysical brothel for her emotions, so I let fly, "If you lost some weight, I bet guys might talk to you." She wasn't fat at all, so I thought she'd get the joke. She didn't. She got mad. I don't know if it's possible to cry without actually shedding tears, but if you can, she definitely did. Hey, if she can't take a joke, fuck her.

I eventually started talking to a very attractive girl about Marley, and his defining characteristic quickly came up:

Tucker "Yeah, he's a good dog. Except that he's profoundly homosexual. He likes to hump male dogs."
Cute Girl "No, he's not gay—it's a dominance thing."
Tucker "It's not a dominance thing. He does other homosexual stuff too. He gossips endlessly about other dogs, watches 'Queer Eye For The Straight Guy', always frets about being skinny enough, and licks his penis constantly. Now you tell me he's not gay."

She thought this was hilarious and introduced me to all her friends. She and all her friends were very attractive, and very cool . . . and very much with their boyfriends, who were all sitting with them. Normally, this would anger me, but the boyfriends thought I was hilarious and kept buying me beers. One of the boyfriends bought a round of shots, and wanted a toast. I don't know why, maybe because I had the dog, maybe because I hadn't paid for shit and they expected something out of me, maybe because I had been entertaining them all night, everyone in this group turned to me to give the toast.

Guy #1 "Hey, Dog Boy, give us a toast!"

This statement was met with cheers from the table.

Tucker "Uhhh . . . OK . . . umm . . . To Marley?"

Booing and hissing rose up through the dozen or so toast participants.

Tucker "I don't know, what kind of toast do you want?"
Guy #2 "A toast. A real toast, something funny."
Guy #1 "Yeah, come on, Dog Boy! You can do it!"

I realize that the boyfriends were trying to make fun of me, setting me up for ridicule to make themselves look better in the eyes of their hot girlfriends. That's fine. I'd have done the same thing. But they obviously didn't know who they were dealing with.

I got up on a chair, and prepared to address the crowd.

Guy #1 "Everyone look, Dog Boy and his mutt are gonna give a toast!"

The room got quiet, I paused for dramatic effect, and gave the only funny toast I know:

"Here's to the women we've met, and to the women we've fucked,
And to those amongst us who've had no such luck.
Here's to beer in the glass, and vodka in the cup,
Here's to pokin' her in the ass, so she won't get knocked up.
Here's to all of you, and here's to me,

Together as friends we'll always be,
But if we should ever disagree,
Then FUCK ALL OF YOU, HERE'S TO ME!"

Not to sound arrogant, but the fucking place erupted. I was a hero.

I wish there was a happy ending to this story, but even after a perfor-mance like that, I still went home alone. Sometimes even Jordan scores 50 and still loses.

UGLY GIRL HITS ON TUCKER, IS DUPED

I'm at the dog park today, and as usual, Marley finds a cute dog and be-gins humping him. No awkward approaches, no expensive dinners, no foreplay, just a few seconds of ass-sniffing and then they start going at it. Dogs have it all figured out.

The dog's owner takes this as a cue to start talking to me. She was, in a word, unattractive. Ugly even. Her dearth of physical beauty did not stop her from aggressively engaging me in conversation. It took about five minutes for me to realize that she was 1) crazy, and 2) in love with me. My favorite quote from her pointless, disjointed ramblings:

UglyGirl "Look at them go at it . . . I haven't done that in a while . . . the last time I got humped like that I was skinny . . . I should start working out again."

I'm at a dog park, an ugly girl is shamelessly hitting on me, and I'm watching my dog ravenously ass-pillage another male dog. So I decide to do the obvious thing, and say the most ridiculous things I can think of, hoping to either entertain myself or get her away from me. The next ten minutes of conversation saw these gems pass my lips:

- "I have a really small penis. At least that's what the priest told me."

- "I like to go to the playground and give candy to children. Just to freak their parents out."

- "I don't have a job. Or even any prospects."

- "I used to be very spiritual. That was until I realized that God makes fun of me behind my back."

- "I'm desperately poor. Could you lend me some money?"

- "It's not like I agree with the Israelis or anything, it's just that I really like the idea of indiscriminately bombing Palestinians."

The hoped-for effect—repulsed horror—was not achieved. In fact, the Gods of Irony struck, and she thought I was hilarious. Uproariously funny. In tears laughing at me. Thanks, but I only hook up with ugly girls when I'm drunk, have no other options, and my friends won't see. Try again later tonight.

DOG PEOPLE DON'T HAVE A
SENSE OF HUMOR

At first Marley's humping was embarrassing, but I've learned to live with it. Sometimes I can even have fun with it. For instance, instead of just profusely apologizing, I've shifted the blame to others. Conversations now go like this:

Tucker "Gosh, I'm really sorry my dog keeps trying to hump your dog. He's normally never like this. Are you putting some kind of canine perfume on your dog?"

Tucker "Maybe your dog is teasing mine. You ever think of that? Your dog does seem to be flaunting its wares a little loosely. What does he expect, sashaying around the dog park like some sort of cheap doggy prostitute?"

Some people laugh, others don't. You'd be surprised how defensive some dog owners get when you tell them their doggy was asking for it.

I eventually figured out one way to REALLY piss off dog people. Say something like this:

Tucker "Sometimes I'll go down to the dog pound and pretend that I found my dog. Then I tell them to kill him anyway, because I already gave away all his stuff."

They get really fucking lit up at that one. Dog people don't have a very good sense of humor.

Dude, we are drinking too much

Occurred, March 2009

One of the cool things about becoming famous—especially for someone in the entertainment business—is getting access to a lot of things few others get: invitations to parties, VIP treatment, gifting suites, you name it. In my case, the coolest thing has been access to sporting events. Not surprisingly, my books have become very popular with pro and college athletes, and I've developed friendships with a bunch of them as a result.

I've become especially good friends with one guy in particular and we've shared some crazy fucking experiences, one of which I have to write about. I promised him I'd never write about him, or even talk about anything we do in any way where he can be identified, so please understand why I'm being vague about certain details: I can't tell you who he is, what team he plays for, or anything like that. What I can tell you is that my friend, "TheWolf," has played big time college and professional basketball for years. He is older now, but he is still in the league. You know who he is.

It was the end of the season and TheWolf was out for the year with a nagging injury, so he could do things he wouldn't normally be able to were he playing in the games. We started the night at his apartment that, of course, is incredible and teeming with women. I had a rental car, so Nils and I gave TheWolf a ride to the game. When we got there, we went past all the awful parking that normal people have to endure, straight into the players' lot, and took the prime spot, literally ten feet from the Players' Entrance.

Tucker "Wolf, you sure I can park here?"

Wolf "Yeah man, this is my spot."

Tucker "But this is my rental car, how are they going to know not to tow it."

Wolf "See those security cameras? They watch everything man, they see me getting out of the car. They won't tow it. I run this place man, relax."

TheWolf took us in the locker room, we met the team, played Madden with everyone, ate at the player buffet, watched shoot-around from the bench, everything. We sat in the incredible seats he provided, watched the game, watched his team blow out the visitor. It was fucking awesome, the type of experience you can't even pay for.

Afterwards everyone was ready to party. The arena Wolf plays in has a restaurant/bar in the bottom that stays open long after the game. After every win, the players get the back room, and the groupies descend. Nils and I had a blast drinking, hanging out, bullshitting and, of course, fucking with all the groupies.

I've said it before, and I'll say it again: As a group, the worst women on earth are LA Girls. But the second worst is very much debatable. I think, as of right now, I may throw my vote to Basketball Groupies. They could be in the top 1% of slimiest, most despicable collection of immoral whores the world has ever known. There's a reason the most popular of all the celebrity wives shows is "Basketball Wives," and why none of them are actually wives anymore. The ones we met that night were so icky, so vile, that I refused to even consider fucking any of them. Not that they even wanted to fuck me—the few that could read and knew who I was, realized quickly that the only thing I'd ever buy them would be an abortion.

As the night wound down, TheWolf, Nils and I got more blitzed. I don't specifically remember leaving the bar, but I do remember us discussing how drunk we were, and how none of us had been that fucked up in a long time. And I also very clearly remember us back in Wolf's apartment, because we stayed up for an hour while one of the groupies made us grilled cheese sandwiches and we had an extended conversation about all the things TheWolf was thinking about doing after his playing career was over. I'm not sure what time we finally went to bed but it was probably somewhere after 3am because when we woke up the next morning to catch our flight we both felt like we'd been hit in the head with a panini press and had our eyes brushed with sandpaper.

We tried to wait for TheWolf to wake up before we left but he was up late having his needs attended to by a different groupie than the one who made us grilled cheese, so we grabbed our luggage and took a taxi over to the arena to pick up the rental car.

Since there was no game that day and the lot was closed, the driver pulled up at the curb outside the ticket plaza. I told him those rules didn't apply to me because I was famous goddamnit, but he was having none of it. Maybe it was because I'm only 6' tall and wearing a filthy shirt from the night before. Maybe it was because he was a filthy illiterate foreigner who didn't know his place. Who's to know? So I paid him and we walked our luggage into the players' parking lot like a couple of normals.

There was no rental car.

Tucker "I fucking knew it!! I knew they were going to tow it! Fucking Wolf!!!"

We only had like two hours before our flight, nowhere near enough time to find the car, pick it up from the impound lot, and drive it back to the airport. Nils called another cab while I called TheWolf's phone and got his voicemail:

Tucker "You stupid drunk broke-kneed motherfucker, I FUCKING TOLD YOU THEY WOULD TOW MY RENTAL CAR!! You better get your worthless fucking assistant to find my car and get it back to the rental place at the airport, I'm not paying a month of rental charges because you 'run that place.' Dumbshit!"

The next day, TheWolf's assistant called the towing companies the stadium uses; none of them towed ANY cars that night. TheWolf himself called all the impound lots the two truck companies use, just in case there was a mix-up. My car wasn't in any of them. In fact, he even went and asked security, and they said they had no record of ANY car being towed from the arena in MONTHS.

The only logical conclusion was that someone had stolen the car out of the players' lot (something that actually happened once at that stadium, like ten years ago), so TheWolf asked the security people to go back and look at all the footage from that night to see if anything showed up, and if it did, to start the process of reporting the car stolen. The next day I got a call from TheWolf:

Wolf "Tucker, I just left the security office. It's a good fucking thing I buy the head of security a bottle of Johnny Walker Blue every year for Christmas, because he just saved my ass from a serious embarrassment in front of the whole organization."
Tucker "What, did someone you know steal the car?"
Wolf "No shithead. You know who drove the car off? WE DID."
Tucker "What?"
Wolf "I just watched the tape. At about 2am, you can clearly see you, me, and Nils walk up to the car, open the doors, get in, and drive the fuck off."
Tucker "What are you talking about?!? We took a cab home!"
Wolf "That's what I thought too!! But we didn't. We drove home!"
Tucker "THAT'S FUCKING IMPOSSIBLE!"
Wolf "TAPE DON'T LIE MOTHERFUCKER!!"
Tucker "Dude . . . we are drinking too much."

Here's the thing: I don't drive drunk. Any more. I did that a few times in my youth, it was stupid and reckless, and I got lucky that nothing really bad ever happened. Then ever since the Absinthe Donuts incident and the Harlem RV incident happened within a few months of each other, I made it a point to never drive drunk again. I stopped cold (wild) turkey.

When Nils and I woke up that morning, I would have bet you $10,000 that we'd taken a taxi home. Nope. Apparently, I DROVE A FUCKING RENTAL CAR back to his place through an unfamiliar city with two or three similarly shit-housed passengers during prime, post-bar DUI hours.

I talked about this with Nils, and he was just as shocked. This whole fucking incident is still baffling to all three of us. Each of us remembers walking out of the bar and discussing who would call to get a taxi. We remember the conversation we had back at TheWolf's place, but not one of the three of us has ANY memory of HOW the fuck we got there. In fact, we don't remember *anything* between those points. It's like that part of the night never happened; like a fucking X-File or something.

IT'S STILL A MYSTERY.

Well, I guess it's not a mystery in the strictest sense, because there is VIDEO TAPE of me, Nils and TheWolf getting into the car and driving it off, and there is a record of the car being towed from out front of The-Wolf's apartment where I forgot/left it.

Like TheWolf says . . . tape don't lie.

I SCORED AT THE SWAMP!!!

Occurred, August 2009

During the months of August, September, and October of 2009, a group of us went on a promotional tour for the movie based on my first book. We did premieres in something like 35 different cities, including many college towns. Of course there were several press things I had to do along the way, and about two weeks before the Gainesville screening, I got this email:

"Hey Tucker,

My name is [redacted] and I am the Director of Cameos for the University of Florida's 2009 Gator Growl show. Gator Growl is the world's largest, entirely student-run pep rally and multimedia event. Attended by more than 70,000 students and Gator fans from all over the country, it is the largest student pep rally in the world, and takes place on the eve of every Florida Homecoming football game at Ben Hill Griffin Stadium in Gainesville.

Celebrity cameos are one of the most prominent parts of the show. Every year, Gator Growl boasts an array of timeless celebrities, athletes, and political figures that appear on video to express their support for the Gator Nation. We would be honored to have you appear in a cameo for this year's Gator Growl. Your cameo would go a long way in helping to make an already prominent reel featuring Bill Clinton, Zach Braff, Chris Collinsworth and Mike Rowe even more prestigious.

Taping a cameo would require no more than 10 minutes of your time. It would consist of you introducing yourself, delivering a personal message to Gator fans, and then ending with the phrase "Let the Gator Growl!" I understand that you will be on campus on August 24th for a showing of your new movie. I will be at the event and we can film the cameo right then and there on a regular camcorder. We would be honored to have you a part of University of Florida history."

Are you fucking shitting me? I am a born and bred UK fan. UF is a hated SEC rival. I would never do something like this.

But it isn't that simple. My hatred for UF is not like my hatred for some other places. I hate Notre Dame because they are the biggest shitheads on earth. Even the real Irish hate the Fighting Irish. And I hate Duke because they are pompous shitbird losers. Not even people in North Carolina like Dukies. And I hate Tennessee because they are redneck, dumbass, low-down dirty snitches.

But UF is different. If I'm really honest with myself, I have to admit that the reason I hate UF is because they ALWAYS BEAT MY BELOVED WILDCATS! As of the writing of this story, they've beaten UK 23 straight fucking times in football. [We kill them in basketball, but we kill everyone in basketball.]

Not only has their football team been dominant for decades, but they've done it in the most frustrating way possible. They embarrass teams. UF has scored 50+ points on more teams than any school in NCAA history. And the whole time they're doing it, they're arrogant, insufferable fucks about it. They're better than us at football, they know it, and every UF fan carries that salt with him, just to rub it in the wounds of other SEC schools. And as if Steve Spurrier and his reign of sarcastic terror weren't bad enough, they had to go and recruit God's other son Tim Tebow, and spend the next decade not just beating everyone in football, but doing it in the most condescending and Christian way possible. They would beat us, then tell us we should drink less. Fuck Steve Spurrier, fuck Tim Tebow, and fuck their awesome football team.

If you remove football from the equation, it becomes much harder to hate UF. I have a ton of really good friends who went there, and every time

I've visited, I've had a great time. A part of me truly wishes I had gone there for undergrad. There's very little not to like about the place. And seriously—how mad can I really get at all those hot, drunk UF girls who want to have sex with me and then feed me fried alligator? If you can be mad at a hot girl who wants to have sex with you—who are you, and what happened to you?

Considering all these things, I tell them yes, I'll do it, but with a condition: I won't say anything bad about UK. They agree, and we set the time to do it right after the screening and before I go out drinking.

They come up to me at the screening, seem like pretty normal nice guys, and we start to shoot it. They tell me what they want me to say, and it's completely ridiculous UF promotional garbage. I counter with something along the lines of, "Fuck off you fucking turd-eating Gators, I hope a plane hits The Swamp."

Shockingly, they aren't too keen on that.

So we go back and forth until we settle on something like, "I am a born and bred Kentucky fan, so I should hate UF . . . but I can't, there are just too many hot girls here. Good luck on your season, except of course, when you play UK." I do a bunch of takes, finally get a good one, and we're golden.

Afterwards, I make a joke about how I should get to fuck a girl on their football field for doing this, as a sort of payment. The guy in charge of the Gator Growl, Tyler, chimes in:

Tyler "Yeah right. That's impossible."
Tucker "You should know that nothing is impossible for Tucker Max."
Tyler "Ben Hill Griffin stadium is locked, and surrounded by huge fences. You can't get in."
Tucker "I'm a good free climber. I can find a way up or around any-thing."

Tyler "And the field itself is guarded 24/7 by security guards. I've tried to fuck on that field for years, and tons of my friends too, and we always get caught."

Tucker "Son . . . I am a legend for a reason. Name the bet."

We make a gentleman's wager, he tells me in the most emphatic terms that there is no chance I'll succeed, and I get on the bus to go over to some bar on campus. It's fucking packed, and I end up drinking right by the front, next to the huge, open, bay windows. After maybe an hour or two, this group of girls walks by me to come in, but the bouncer won't let them. Apparently the girl is 19.

TallSlut "Tucker Max! Can you get me in please!"

Tucker "How old are you?"

TallSlut "19."

Tucker "Are you kidding or stupid?"

TallSlut "But I went to your movie tonight and I want to come hang out with you."

Tucker "Honey I'm awesome, but even I can't fight city hall on this."

I start bullshitting with her, and she makes it pretty clear she wants to fuck me. OK cool, but I'm having fun at the bar, and she's cute, but not so hot that I can't stop myself from leaving immediately, so whatever. Then Bill Dawes makes the obvious connection that I missed:

Bill "Dude, I bet she'll fuck you on the field. Try it."

I go outside the bar, find her, and make it real clear:

Tucker "You wanna fuck, right?"

TallSlut "Yeah, of course."

Tucker "OK, I'll fuck you, but only if we fuck on the field in The Swamp."

TallSlut "Deal. I go to UCF, I hate them."

Jackpot!

To avoid redundancy, I'll just print what I wrote on the movie blog the next day:

"No matter what else happens on this tour, with this movie, or in my life, I don't care. I can die happy, because last night I did what no other Kentuckian has done in years: I scored at The Swamp.

I mean this literally. I snuck into the stadium, with a girl, and fucked her on the goal line of the south end zone. Right below the goal posts, underneath the national championship signs.

If this gets me in trouble, I don't care. If the Gainesville PD puts out a warrant for my arrest for some bullshit misdemeanor, so be it, I will turn myself in and deal with it. If it means I get banned from UF, that would suck, but those are consequences I will live with.

No matter what happens, it will all be worth it. Now every time I watch UF play, even though goddamn Tim Tebow may be unstoppable, even though UF has more team speed than a pack of cheetahs and destroys my beloved Wildcats every year, I now know that they have to cross the place where I had sex with a girl to do it. I defiled their shire. It'll never be the same.

To every other team in the SEC: You are welcome to bask in the glow of this score also, because it will probably be the only one any of us get on UF this year.

And to the UF community: I'm sorry. I still love you guys, I really do, but it had to be done. Might as well be me.

And of course I have pics, because without those, I know all the butthurt Gators would try to call BS:

Redacted, because she's nice

The response came almost immediately. One of my good friends, TheGeneralsDaughter, is a proud UF alum, and when I told him what we did, he flipped shit:

"I hope your bus flips over 17 times and explodes into a churning inferno of God's special brand of hatred. Hate is too poor a word for my feelings toward you right now."

My response: "ON THE GOAL LINE!!"

Him: "Fuck. You. You are dead to me!"

I emailed the pictures to Tyler:

"I'm speechless. That tall blonde slut was sitting behind me during the Q and A. I think I saw her after, if I'm thinking the right girl. That story on your site probably made for better publicity for your movie than the actual movie premiere in Gainesville."

Now, I knew this would get responses like that from people I knew. But what I didn't anticipate is what Tyler said—this act got more press than the movie premiere itself. Like 25 media outlets picked this story up. Some examples:

From *The Gainesville Sun:*

> Blogger Claims He Snuck into UF Stadium for Sex
> August 25th, 2009
> by Nathan Crabbe
>
> A blogger known for writing about his sexual exploits has made Ben Hill Griffin Stadium the site of another notch on his belt.
>
> Tucker Max, whose book is the basis of a new movie, posted a blog entry Tuesday claiming he snuck into the stadium after the movie's Gainesville premiere and had sex in the south end zone. He posted pictures of him and the woman, who isn't identified, standing in the stadium as proof they were there.
>
> Max's book, *I Hope They Serve Beer in Hell,* is basis of a new movie. It was shown Monday night in Gainesville as part of a 31-city tour leading up to its national premiere next month.

———————

On the blog, he wrote that he "will turn (himself) in and deal with it" if a warrant for his arrest is issued.

University of Florida Police Sgt. Stephen Wilder said such an incident could lead to trespassing or lewd and lascivious charges if the couple was caught in the act, but nothing would likely be done now.

"It's certainly not something that the department would pursue after the fact," he said.

Reached by phone, Max said he got the idea to sneak into the stadium from a UF student filming him for this year's Gator Growl. He said he climbed a fence to get into the stadium around midnight.

From *The GainesVillians:*

This brings up the struggle between respect & hate. Where one must respect one's effort in successfully pulling out any random sex act in The Ben Hill Griffin Stadium aka "The Swamp" or any other public space. But where as being a Gator, hating him for disgracing our beloved field with his corrosive semen.

From *Banned in Hollywood:*

Gives new meaning to hitting the tight end across the middle. Kudos to Mr. Max for doing more than the Sooners could muster in last year's National Championship Game. We can only imagine that Lane Kiffin and his ridiculously hot wife are next to attempt this, recruiting violations be damned.

But my personal favorite is what **Drew Franklin from KentuckySports Radio.com** (the biggest UK sports blog) said:

What has Tim Tebow not done at Florida? He has two national championships and a Heisman trophy, he's a two time All-American, *GQ* cover model, number one image in the Urban Meyer spank bank, and captain/leader of the soon-to-be 2010 National Champions. He has done it all . . . well, almost. He has never had sex with a girl on the goal line at Ben Hill Griffin Stadium (or in a bed for that matter). Florida, we see your Tebow and we raise you our Tucker Max . . .

Take that, Florida. I don't even care what the scoreboard says when you come to Commonwealth on September 26th. In my mind, we've already won. Tucker, I think I speak for all of Big Blue Nation when I say, thank you. Thank you for being a Wildcat.

TUCKER GOES TO DOCTOR, HILARITY ENSUES

Occurred, May 2010

I wrote a story in *Assholes Finish First* called "The Tucker Max SeX-ray" about going on "Loveline" and shocking Dr. Drew with video of me getting a blowjob in a running x-ray machine. [You can see it at **www.tuckermax .com /sexray**]. I went back on "Loveline" in January 2010 to promote that book, actually, and the show went great as always, because Dr. Drew is awesome. During one of the breaks, we talked again about the SeX-ray video, and he asked me if I had gotten a check-up like he recommended during my previous appearance.

Tucker "What do you mean? Like seen a doctor? No."
Dr. Drew "You really should."
Tucker "I have felt a little, I don't know—less like myself recently."
Nils "You sound like a fucking anti-depressant ad."
Dr. Drew "You really should get checked out. Shooting that much radiation across your balls can affect testosterone, which would explain that."

I ignore the vast majority of what people say to me, both good and bad, and I can't remember the last time I took advice from someone. But I respect the hell out of Dr. Drew, even more so now that I kinda know him in real life. When he tells me to do something, especially something medical, I pay attention.

I don't really trust most doctors though, so when I got back to Austin, I found a blood testing facility and got my own lab tests done. They came back and confirmed what Dr. Drew had suspected: I had really low testosterone. It was right at the lower bound of normal, which put it about half of what I was at the last time I got full blood work done. This is not good. I immediately found a highly recommended endocrinologist (a doctor that specializes in hormones), and made an appointment. She was supposed to be "the best" in central Texas.

It's funny—when doctors are considered "the best" it usually means one of two things: They really are awesome, or they are all hype and really fucking suck. It became immediately clear which one this was.

The doctor came into the exam room an hour late. She was about mid-forties, definitely pretty, but in a severe way. She carried herself with an air that immediately said, "I am such a delicate genius, you're lucky to be in my presence." That was the first bad sign. She started off by recapping what I'd told her receptionist when I made the appointment.

DoctorUppity "So, it says here you *think* you have low testosterone?"
Tucker "Yeah, well I have been feeling kinda sluggish and tired and, it's hard to describe, but just not myself recently. Like I am a step behind who I normally am. I'm pretty sure my low testosterone is the cause."
DoctorUppity "Well, we don't actually know if you have low testosterone, we'll have to run some tests, and then—"
Tucker "Oh no, I do. I already did them."

I handed her my blood test results, as well as some from two years ago that showed a baseline for me. I thought she'd be excited about this, that a patient had taken an interest in his health and done some of her work for her.

DoctorUppity "You ALREADY did blood tests? How? Where?"

She wasn't asking me because she was confused. She was asking me, incredulous, like she was mad at me.

Tucker "At a place called Any Lab Test Now. They draw your blood and send it off for tests to the same labs the doctors do. Here are the results."

She snatched the papers from my hand and started rifling through them, as if they were scientific poison. Now I know what Galileo felt like. She started lecturing me about patients thinking they know better than doctors, and about how I wasn't qualified to read and interpret the results—even though these are the exact same results that get sent to doctors. She had a "I am the sole expert here because I gave the University of Texas $130k and 4 years of my life" attitude was a REALLY bad sign. Experts who think they hold a monopoly on knowledge within their subject or field are not only usually bad at their jobs, they can be dangerous (e.g., the cause of the 2008 financial crash). I could talk for hours about why this is the case, but you probably don't care, because it's not funny (if you do care, go read *The Black Swan* by Nassim Taleb, or Seth Roberts' blog).

DoctorUppity "Why did you do this?"
Tucker "Do what?"
DoctorUppity "Get your own blood tests done?"
Tucker "How else am I going to see if there's a problem?"
DoctorUppity "Well, you can come to the doctor first, like everyone else."

I probably should have just walked out at that point. This woman was obviously a fucking disaster. But I didn't. I was desperate to fix my balls.

Tucker "I kinda did. I'm here because Dr. Drew told me to come."
DoctorUppity "Dr. Drew?"
Tucker "You know, from 'Loveline' and 'Celebrity Rehab,' and—"
DoctorUppity "Oh, I KNOW who Dr. Drew is. What does he have to do with why you're here?"
Tucker "Well, when I was on his show—"
DoctorUppity "You called into '*Loveline*' for *medical* advice?"

Her tone was about as condescending and rude as it could get for a service provider speaking to a paying client. She may have been questioning my intelligence for calling in to a radio show for medical advice, which I guess I can understand. But in the moment, I took it like she was questioning Dr. Drew's credibility as a doctor. That was basically the tipping point for me. I turned combative and sarcastic.

Tucker "No, I did not. I was a guest on the show."

DoctorUppity "You were a guest on 'Loveline'?"

Tucker "Yes, and when I told Dr. Drew what happened to me, he told me to get checked out."

DoctorUppity "What happened?"

Tucker "Well, I got a blowjob in front of an X-ray machine."

DoctorUppity "You're kidding right?"

Tucker "I think if you saw the video, it would clear everything up."

DoctorUppity "The video?"

There wasn't a computer in the exam room, so I walked out to the reception area. This office had multiple doctors in it, so there was not just a solo receptionist sitting at the front desk. There was also a handful of nurses and techs milling around. Before the doctor could really figure out what was going on, I got in front of the computer, typed "Tucker Max SeX-ray" into Google, and clicked on the video.

I hadn't watched this video in a long time, and I'd forgotten that it had music to it. In fact, if you are at a computer, go bring up the video and make sure the sound is on. Well, that computer had the sound on too. Loud. Which made everything even more awesome.

DoctorUppity "Is that . . . are you . . . oh my God . . ."

Now it's time for the tables to turn on this doctor. The sound to the video, combined with her reaction, pretty much ensured everyone in the office came over to see what was going on. And of course, I am never one to not play to a crowd.

Tucker "The video is exactly what I told you it was—me getting a blowjob in front of an X-ray machine."

DoctorUppity "WHY WOULD YOU DO THAT? DO YOU HAVE ANY IDEA HOW DANGEROUS THAT IS??"

Tucker "Well, I wanted to invent a new genre of porn."

DoctorUppity "You wanted to invent a new genre of porn???"

At this point, the whole thing turned into a fucking Abbott and Costello "Who's on First?" routine.

DoctorUppity "WHO ARE YOU??"

Tucker "Tucker Max."

Tech "You're Tucker Max? Really?"

Nurse "Hey, I read your book. You're that buttsex guy! You're so funny!"

DoctorUppity "You know who he is?"

Receptionist "Of course, he's like, famous or something. Right?"

Tucker "Are you asking me if I'm famous?"

DoctorUppity "You're famous? For blowjob videos?"

Tech "I've seen that. I remember when that video came out!"

Tucker "Hi, nice to meet you."

DoctorUppity "I still don't understand how you even did this. Using a fluoroscope like this is highly illegal."

Tucker "Well, it was the X-ray tech who was the one giving me the blow-job."

Tech "Yeah, I read that in your book. That was hilarious."

DoctorUppity "This is in a book? You wrote a book?"

Nurse "Yeah, I read it. It was funny. This wasn't in the book though, was it?"

Tech "Yeah, it was in his second book."

Nurse "You have two books?!? How did I miss that? What's it called?"

Tucker "*Assholes Finish First.*"

Receptionist "They sure do."

Nurse "Oh my God, I have to go get a copy!"

Tech "Yo, can I get a picture with you? My friend is never going to believe this. You're his hero."

Tucker "Of course."

It took like ten minutes to get back on track after that. I had to backtrack and explain everything again to the doctor, who was in such shock she almost couldn't process it. I mean, in her defense—this video shocked Dr. Drew, so her being really fucked up over it is understandable.

There isn't much else to talk about for this story, at least anything else that's funny. Her medical advice was for me to go on hormone therapy. What a fucking quack—I'm a healthy 35-year-old; I'm not taking synthetic hormones for the rest of my life. I never went back to her.

I can happily report that my testosterone is now better than ever, because with the help of a few very smart people (not doctors), I figured out a way to fix it naturally using mega-dosing of certain vitamins and certain specific dietary and lifestyle changes. But that is a long, long story, and definitely not one that is entertaining enough to tell in this book.

THE BLOWJOB INTERLUDES

PART 1

Occurred, May 2007

So this girl I've been fucking for a while is at my place right now, and really wants to be in my next book. I explained to her that, at this point in my life, the bar is pretty high to do something noteworthy enough to get a story written about you, and not only that, but you probably don't want to be in a story—they tend to be about shitty things that happen, either to me or to the girl.

But she is a nice, fun girl, and not only very hot, but very persuasive. Since there is nothing noteworthy to write about her . . .

I had her fellate me while I typed this.

So there you go honey, now you're in my book. Congrats.

[Updated after she left: The fact that I could type that without making any mistakes should tell you the quality of the fellatio. Hot girls are almost never good at head; they don't have to be. But still, a nice girl, and I promised her I'd keep it in, so here it is.]

PART 2

Occurred, August 2007

Same thing as before, just a different girl. I'm going to make this my default response from now on when a girl asks to be in one of my books. Such a beautifully elegant and orgasmic solution to an annoyingly persistent problem.

This girl's pretty good, I'm cutting this short to focus.

PART 3

Occurred, January 2008

Again. I wonder what they are all going to do when they read this? Probably bitch and complain and send me long emails that I will ignore about how unique and special they are. None of them so far have asked if they are the only one, and the first one was the only one who actually wanted to see what I wrote.

I'm starting to think they may care less about what I say about them, and more about bragging to their friends that they're in a book.

PART 4

Occurred, July 2008

I posted this on Twitter when it happened. All from the same girl:

———

Post #1:

@TuckerMax
Tucker Max ✓

Her "Write about me!" Me "U aren't interesting. Except for your mouth." Her "I'll blow you while you twitter!" She's doing a good job

29 Jul 09 via web   ☆ Favorite ⇄ Retweet ↩ Reply

Post #2:

@TuckerMax
Tucker Max ✓

But not so good that I can't type. The biggest room is the room for improvement, right, top of her head? I think she's nodding yes.

29 Jul 09 via web   ☆ Favorite ⇄ Retweet ↩ Reply

Post #3:

@TuckerMax
Tucker Max ✓

Her "OMG! So funny! Link my twitter account!" Me "You weren't that good." Her "Practice makes perfect." Perseverance is sexy

29 Jul 09 via web   ☆ Favorite ⇄ Retweet ↩ Reply

THE RIMJOB INTERLUDE

Occurred, December 2009

This one did ask and did want to see what I wrote, so I showed her the series of past Blowjob Interludes. Of course she wants to be different . . .

So she's eating out my ass as I type this. This is awkward, on my hands and knees, typing with someone's tongue in my shit pipe. But I have to admit, it's nice. Nice enough that I typed all fucked up.

[Edit: I was going to leave it that way as a testament to her ability, but she is one of those anal grammar Nazis and corrected everything in "her" story.]

[Edited after she left: I am pretty sure I showered since my last crap, but she didn't ask. Weird; usually the type of girl who is an anal grammar nerd is also afraid of poop. Whatever. I've stopped thinking I know anything about women any more. The more you think you know, the less you actually do. I think Einstein said that. I don't know, but whoever said it, I bet my asshole is shinier than his right now.]

PART 5

Occurred, May 2010

Had another want to be in a book. I showed her this series of vignettes, she read them, and like most girls, demanded that she do something "new and different." Nothing is new, honey; the Romans did it all and more two thousand years ago, but whatever.

I told her the best way to be different was to act like she was emotionally stable. She waved that off quickly. I made some other suggestions—I type while she cleans my place, I type while she makes me dinner—she didn't like any of them. She wanted it to be sexual. I suggest I do her from behind, and set my computer on her back and type while I am inside her. Not "baller" enough for her. Then, she lit up with excitement:

Girl "I know! I will fuck you in the ass, and you can write about that?"
Tucker "Yeah right. Next idea."
Girl "I'm serious! I even have one in my car."
Tucker "Have what?"
Girl "My dildo!"
Tucker "You ride around with your dildo . . . in your car?"
Girl "Not just my dildo, I think I have the whole strap-on belt too."
Tucker [flabbergasted] "Are you fucking serious?"
Girl "What? I do it to guys all the time."

I stared at her for a second, assuming she was kidding and would say so. Nope.

Girl "You know you want to do it."
Tucker "You can leave now."
Girl "Don't be a pussy!"

I went straight old-school Eddie Murphy on her:

Tucker "Get the fuck out of my motherfucking house!"

THE FAT GIRL LEFTOVERS

Whenever something happens to me that could be a funny story, I try to write down as many notes and quotes as I can. Most of the time I do a good job with my notes. Not always.

I intended to put the two stories below into the *Hilarity Ensues* story, "Fat girls cross Tucker, hilarity ensues," but I cut both because of memory/recall/notes issues.

Though I have the "Fat AND Racist" notes as being a single conversation with one obnoxious fat girl, I am not confident that it was. I definitely remember the fat girl the story is about, but my notes aren't totally clear that all of those jokes are from our interaction with her. We fucked with a lot of people that weekend, and both of us were VERY drunk the whole time. I know all that shit was said, but I may be getting something basic like who it was said to wrong, so I decided to put it in here.

"The Tucker Max Diet" is fucked up for one specific reason: for the fucking life of me, I cannot remember what I said in the most important exchange in the story (you'll understand as you read it). My buddy who was there with me that night doesn't remember it either, and I can't find the girl. Great.

Fat AND Racist

Occurred, April 2007

One time I was hanging out with my buddy Junior, and we were at a bar to meet some girls, when I accidentally bumped into a girl and spilled her drink all over her hand. It was my fault, so without paying much mind to the whole thing, I quickly apologized and offered to buy her another round. Usually people in this situation are gracious and cool, and they thank you and get back to whatever it was they were previously doing. Not this girl.

Girl "Uhhh . . . you can do better than that."

The temerity of her tone pulled my head around in her direction like my dog when she hears the word "treat." What I saw threw me for a total loop.

Now, understand, comparing fat girls is a lot like a Turd Beauty Pageant— no matter who wins, it's still a piece of shit—but while this girl was not the most disgusting fat girl I've ever met in my life, she could have been on stage with her. She was 5'8", maybe 230 pounds, with a tight red shirt that forced her fat rolls out over the waistband of her way-too-tight jeans, like the worst muffin top you could imagine. She had that white trash kind of bad skin complete with the type of low-level acne people get when they eat too much junk food. She looked like a red velvet cupcake with butterface icing.

Tucker "Do better than what?"
Fat Girl "Do a better job than that trying to pick me up."

I turn to look at Junior, to get confirmation that she actually said that. He shook his head in dismay. Everything went off the wheels from there:

Junior "Oh no."

Tucker "What did you just say?"

Fat Girl "I said that was a lame attempt to pick me up."

Tucker "I'm sorry, please say that again one more time, because I want to be very sure about what you said. I'd feel bad if this was a mistake."

Junior [to the fatty] "If you want to like yourself in the morning, you won't answer that."

Fat Girl "I SAID that your attempt to pick me up was bad, and that you should try again with something better."

I stared at her in disbelief and shock. Not only did I not own a forklift, but she was so fat, and so ugly, and such a disaster in every way . . . it was like when a crazy person talks such intense nonsense that for a second, you begin to think you're the crazy one. For a brief moment, I actually questioned myself, trying to see the angle she was seeing that I HAD to be missing.

Then I realized she wasn't seeing anything I was missing; she was just a fat fucking idiot. Thus began one of the most ridiculously hilarious and insane exchanges I've ever had in my entire life:

Tucker "You're right; I do find you attractive."

Fat Girl "I know; that's why you're trying to talk to me."

Tucker "Yep, and I want to sleep with you."

Fat Girl "Oh, I know."

Tucker "But . . . I want to wait."

Fat Girl "For what?"

Tucker "For the version of you that's not disgustingly fat."

Fat Girl "I'm hot."

Junior "Hot? You mean the temperature is high, that's why you're sweating so much, right?"

Tucker [bar whisper to Junior] "Junior, shut up, you're blowing it! You never get to see marine mammals up close like this." [Back to her] "Can I see your propeller scars?"

Fat Girl "Whatever, there are plenty of guys who are into me."

Tucker "Oh no doubt. In fact, I know the perfect guy for you. You've probably heard of him; he's famous. His name is Hagrid."

Fat Girl "Hagrid? Who is that?"

Tucker "You're fat AND illiterate!?! You just keep getting better!"

I would tell you that this was the point when the bartender brought her some fried appetizer she ordered, but that's not true. He brought TWO plates over. After that, we had to keep talking to her to see if she was even real.

Junior "I bet 90% of the guys that hit on you are black, aren't they?

Fat Girl "I do love the dark meat."

Tucker "I think you like every type of meat."

Junior "For real—you don't think that says something about your weight?"

Fat Girl "I like it. You know the saying, 'Once you go black, you never go back.'"

Tucker "No, you have it wrong. The saying is 'If you're fat, you HAVE to go black . . . and because of that, we don't WANT you back.'"

Junior [aside to me] "You've slept with black girls."

Tucker "It's different. Black girls can be really hot."

Fat Girl "You're just jealous of black guys. Your dick is too small to handle this much woman."

Tucker "So is a freight elevator. I'm in good company."

Fat Girl "Well I know plenty of black guys that can handle it. I always pick the black guy."

Junior "Pick? Like, from different choices?"

Tucker "You're saying MORE than one person wants to have sex with you?"

Fat Girl "A bunch of guys tried to fuck me last night."

Junior "I'll believe anything now."

Tucker "Wait—back up. You give preference to black guys over other types of guys who hit on you? I don't think this is the kind of affirmative action Thurgood Marshall was fighting for."

Eventually, she tried to play the standard trump card, even though it's not really in her deck:

Fat Girl "You're a racist."

Tucker "I'm racist!?! I choose who to have sex with based on what they are like as a person. You're the one who picks which guys to fuck BASED ON THEIR SKIN COLOR! That is the very definition of racism, which makes YOU the racist, not me."

Fat Girl "Like I said, you're just jealous."

Tucker "OF WHAT??? YOU'RE FAT, UGLY, ILLITERATE, STUPID AND RACIST! AND A BITCH!"

Junior "This is almost impressive. It's like reality has no meaning to her."

Where do these people that lack such basic self-awareness come from? It's not like this shit is unique to her. That's the whole premise of shows like "Jersey Shore"—that it's fun to watch idiots who don't realize they are idiots. But seriously—where the fuck do they come from? What factors produce these people?

Whatever it is, I have to give Fat Girl a lot of credit—nothing we said had any effect on her. It wasn't like she was employing some kind of sophisticated psychological defense mechanism she'd developed over the years. Words simply didn't register with her. Maybe there is something to the idea of being so stupid that you don't even know how stupid you are.

THE TUCKER MAX DIET

Occurred, June 2003

If you read *Assholes Finish First,* you remember SippyCup. He's the guy who sent me that long email telling me about how I was his hero, the guy who got his nickname because he kept dropping his beer, and we made him start drinking out of an actual sippy cup. That guy. Well, I know I made him out to be a kind of pussy . . . and that's because he is one. A good guy and a lovable pussy, but a pussy nonetheless.

There are some things about him that defy his normal pussy behavior, however. Like his angry, insane hatred of fat girls. "Insane hatred" might not be a strong enough description. I've seen him foaming at the mouth screaming at a random fat girl who did absolutely nothing to him, except be fat in his presence. For whatever reason—I'm guessing childhood rejection— when faced with a fat girl, his seething anger trumps his fear, and he flips out on her.

Most of the time when he flips out on a fat girl, he crosses the line with that shit, and goes from funny to lame before you can blink. Funny requires intelligence and mental dexterity: it's not about hurting the person, it's about finding the humor in the situation. SippyCup doesn't care about creative put-downs or witty insults; he wants to find the quickest path to complete dehumanization. He just recklessly dives into the soul of fat girls and stabs them repeatedly with the red-hot pokers of his outrage and disdain. It's almost never funny.

But sometimes it is. Especially when the girl comes back at him.

One of these times was in 2003. I was hanging out with Sippy in Austin, Texas, and some girls who read my website and loved it wanted to come hang out with us. I can't remember if I looked at pics of them or not, but this was 2003—long before I had enough girls asking to come fuck me that I was rejecting many—so I doubt I did, and I thus don't think I warned Sippy that one of the girls coming out would be fat.

Two girls showed up. One was pretty hot, and one had a nice face, but was fat (Pamela). Not obese, but definitely overweight. A borderline boom boom fatty. Sippy was aghast, and pulled me aside.

Sippy "Tucker, I can't believe you let a fat girl come hang out."
Tucker "I don't care; I'm fucking her friend. She seems OK though."
Sippy "What am I supposed to do?"
Tucker "Jump on the grenade."
Sippy "WHAT?!? SHE'S FAT!!"

Tucker "Dude, just get real drunk, then find something redeeming about her, and focus on that."

Sippy looked at me like I'd just described the grand unifying theory to him. I guess the idea that you could talk to fat girls without berating them was new to him.

He tried this for a while. Listening to his halting, almost farcical attempts to talk to her like a normal person was high comedy. It was like watching two people who don't speak the same language try to communicate. And they're both retarded.

Confident that my sage advice had won the day, I went to the bathroom . . . and returned to find him already neck deep in argument:

Sippy "No, you're wrong. Being fat IS the worst thing a person can be. Much worse than being a murderer."

Here we go.

If you're a fat girl, the best tactic to use against Sippy when he says stupid shit like this is to not engage him on the fat issue, but instead attack him back. I mean, he tries so hard, bless his heart—but at the end of the day, he's still a skinny, dorky, insecure nerd with a nose that would give Toucan Sam beak envy. If you redirect the conversation to his faults, and you're smart about it, you can generally overwhelm him.

Unfortunately, Pamela let Sippy define the boundaries of their conversation—fat—and engaged him there. Which of course brought out angry, "I hate fat girls" Sippy, and he spent the next hour making abusive, ad hominem attacks. Most were stupid, but this girl was SUCH a glutton for punishment that he got a few funny ones in:

Sippy "What did you have for lunch?"
Pamela "Well, I had—"
Sippy "IT WAS TOO MUCH."

Pamela "What?"

Sippy "I think you have some of it still on your chin. Oh, wait, no—it's just your other chin."
Pamela "Oh, I get it. Very original."

Sippy "There's no reason for you to open your mouth. There's no cake here."
Pamela "Ha. Ha. I've heard them all."

Sippy "It's a good thing you're fat, actually. You keep thousands of people in the junk food industry employed. If you went on a diet, McDonald's would go out of business."
Pamela "I don't eat McDonald's."
Sippy "Then why do you look like a fire hydrant? If you were red, dogs would piss on you. Why can't you be anorexic like all the other girls I'd rather have sex with? It worked for Tracey Gold and Karen Carpenter."
Pamela "Isn't Karen Carpenter dead?"
Sippy "Better than being fat!"
Pamela "Uh, not really."
Sippy "What possible benefits do you think there are to being fat?!?"

It was clear that the only reason she couldn't come back at Sippy effectively was because she really was insecure about her weight, and he was ruthlessly hitting that nerve. It wasn't until this exchange that I had any idea how bad it would be:

Tucker "Why don't you two just fuck and get it over with?"
Sippy "I'd never fuck her!"
Pamela "I wouldn't fuck you if you were the last person on earth!"
Sippy "If we were the last two people on earth, you'd probably eat me!"
Pamela "I don't get you. Look around here—there are fat girls everywhere, are there not? Obesity is normal in America."
Sippy "No, being fat is not OK. Society doesn't like fat people. Look at *Maxim.*"
Tucker "Society? Sippy, shut the fuck up. You're one to talk. People who

live in glass houses shouldn't throw stones. Especially when those glass houses let us see how stupid and awkward you look all the time. Do I need to point out that you look like an anorexic flamingo? I'd plant you in my front yard to scare away all the other birds if I wasn't worried your ugly fucking face would lower the property value. Don't let me get started, I will ride you like a rented mule."

Pamela broke up laughing as Sippy meekly dipped his head, like a whipped puppy.

Tucker "And *Maxim*? Really? You're telling me that because some gay art director at some crappy magazine likes photoshopped pictures of waifish girls that remind him of little boys, it means society wants girls to look like concentration camp victims? Fuck that. Even I reject that shit."
Pamela "Thank you!"
Tucker "Hold on, you're still fat. Let's put Sippy's juvenile bullshit to the side for a second, and actually look at the issues here: Do you think you're overweight? Honestly."
Pamela "Yes."
Tucker "OK, fair enough. But here's the important issue: Do you really care? At the end of the day, it's your life, not mine or Sippy's or anyone else's. You're right, you are objectively overweight, but if you're fine with how you are, fuck everyone else's opinion."
Pamela "No, I don't like my weight."
Tucker "OK, that's fine. Pericles said, 'There is no shame in poverty, there is only shame in not taking action to escape from it.' If you don't like your weight, why haven't you done anything to change it?"
Pamela "I have."
Tucker "Really?"
Pamela "I tried the South Beach Diet."
Tucker "The South Beach Diet? That's heroin and champagne. It only works if you want to end up a strung-out junkie. You haven't done shit have you?"
Pamela "I've done other things too!"

Pamela kinda took a breath to respond, and I gave her a "don't bullshit me" look that forced her eyes down toward the floor in knowing shame.

Tucker "You need to go on The Tucker Max Diet. It's a very simple combination of introspection, honest self-evaluation, and action."

[This is the part I don't have any notes for, and I can't fucking remember what I said to her. It wasn't even that amazing of a speech to me that I remembered it or even thought to take notes; I think it was about twenty minutes of pretty simple analysis of her life choices that led to pretty obvious conclusions. I really wish I could remember it, because it would make her subsequent email to me so much better. Whatever it was I said, she ended up so fucking scrambled that a while later, we saw her eating bar fruit. Seriously—she was chowing on martini olives and maraschino cherries. It was awesome.]

Sippy "I've never seen a girl eat bar fruit before! You're in her head!"
Tucker "Maybe she's just hungry. Offer to get her some food."
Sippy "Where I am going to find a whole cow at this hour?!?!?"

The rest of the night was not eventful. A week or so later, Pamela sent me this email:

"I know you get this all the time, but here it is from me:

I know you boast about the 'destruction left in your wake,' but I can say that the experience of meeting you last week has been a positive one for me. I assumed the risk for everything that took place and I am dealing with that. I am dealing in that I am working to be different. I am starting Weight Watchers, for one. I am not doing it so that I can be more attractive to you and your cronies, but I am doing it because I will never attain the level of respect that I want and deserve if people perceive me as being negligent when it comes to maintaining myself.

Alcohol is my demon. I will never be respected so long as I am allowing my personal affairs to be jeopardized by my drunken foolish behavior. Every once and a while is one thing, but I have been living a VERY unhealthy lifestyle void of balance for the past year.

If you were just a drunk, the story would be different. Any dumbass can get drunk and tell funny stories—you've got something else. I mean, here I am telling you how addicted I have become to your presence that I am having difficulty pulling away—and this is after being publicly embarrassed (although that could have been way worse . . . thanks for that).

I suppose my point here is the ultimate irony of the situation: On one level, you take pride in destruction of other people; on my level, your propensity for destruction has altered my life habits for the better. Here's the thing I was missing, and I think most people miss: It's not a malicious destruction. It's a creative destruction. You are a complete dick, yes, but you're also a truth teller. Everyone else is so fake and lies to your face and pretends what's plain as day doesn't exist. You just stand up and say that the emperor has no clothes.

I will continue to be fascinated by who you are and I look forward to watching how you evolve. I hope to continue learning from you in the same ironic way I have thus far. I hope to maintain contact with you and I trust that if you decide to publish this email, I trust you will edit in good taste— well, I hope so anyways."

GIRL DETERMINED TO FUCK TUCKER

Occurred, June 2003

My buddy Ryan and I began this night at some shitty bar having $1 You-Call-It. A $25 tab later, I called it Getting Real Drunk.

I don't remember much, but I do know that my time in the bar was a success, mainly because there were at least eight girls pissed at me and half a dozen guys who wanted to kick my ass. I do remember this one ugly monster acting like a bitch and pissing me off. Someone had to put her in her place—who better than me?

Tucker "Do you have a pen?"
Girl "No. Why?"
Tucker "I want to get your autograph."
Girl "Who do you think I look like?"
Tucker "The Incredible Hulk."
Girl "OH MY GOD!"

Her fat friend made the unfortunate mistake of coming to her defense.

Fat girl "How could you say that? I think she is very good looking."
Tucker "Are you kidding? I can't even feel my eyes anymore."
Fat girl "What a fucking asshole!"

This particular fat girl apparently was a big fan of the Navy, because she had on this weird looking quasi-sailor suit that was way too tight for her.

Tucker "Ahoy, set sails for the Port of Mayonnaise! Petty Officer Puddingtime is out of Oreos!"

Fat Girl "You can't say that!"

Tucker "I can't? I just did. You mean I shouldn't?"

Fat Girl "No, I mean—"

Tucker "It doesn't matter, you aren't hot enough to talk to me."

Fat Girl "Yeah, well YOU aren't hot enough to talk to ME!"

Tucker "OK, if I'm not hot enough, then why are you still talking to me? Shouldn't you be with the hot people? Oh wait, that's me. Go on, the uglies are over there waiting for you. They saved you a spot under the table."

Fat Girl "Fuck you!"

Tucker "So you ready to get out of here?"

Fat Girl "What! I would never hook up with you!"

Tucker "Hook up? No, no. I need to plant some corn, and with those shoulders you have to be able to pull the shit out of a plow."

Needless to say, when 2am comes and everyone has to leave the bar, I am without female accompaniment. Outside, I notice this hot girl staring at me. Just fucking around, I point at her and motion for her to come over to me. She does. Then she starts talking to me like she knows me. Fine with me, whatever turns her on, right?

Not even two minutes later I suggest she get into a cab with me, she agrees and as we are waving one down, three of her friends rush over and pull her away, castigating her for almost leaving with me.

How weird was this? Whatever, I just ignore them. It's never good style to sweat pussy. Nothing smells worse to a woman than desperation. Plus, I don't really give a shit either way.

I look over about three minutes later, and no surprise, she is staring at me again. I smile, she smiles, and I motion for her to come back over. She walks right to me, but once again, her friends follow her over and try to pull her away.

Ryan tries to intervene like a wingman should, but there was nothing he could do. It was like one man trying to block the entire Baltimore Ravens defensive line: he didn't have a chance. The girls swarmed around him and attacked me.

The girl hugged on my arm while her friends pulled on her and yelled at her to get away from me. I half-heartedly tried to make fun of them— "Shouldn't you worry more about that muffin top spilling out over your jeans and less about her sex life?"—but they eventually won. They had to peel her hands off of me finger by finger—she was holding on that tight—but they did manage to pry her away from me.

They carry her—literally pick her up and carry her—to another taxi. Ryan and I are laughing at this scene, though I'm slightly pissed about losing such an easy thing. Of course, I didn't have to work for it, but still—found money is always the best. They push her into the back seat of a taxi, and then pile in after her. Then we witness one of the most miraculous things I've ever seen:

She climbs across the back seat, opens the other side door, and steps out. Her friend who got into the cab after her lunges across the seat at her, grabs hold of her shirt, but the girl pulls her shirt, breaks free, and SPRINTS over to me.

I am in shock. The scene looks like a Benny Hill skit. I have never seen any girl NEED to get to me this badly. I couldn't have thrown a boomerang and had it come back to me any faster.

I immediately grab her, hop into a cab, and laugh as her friends, who are running after the cab screaming, trying to wave it down.

We had lots of drunk sex, and the girl left in the morning.

Tucker Max: 1
Cock-blocking bitches: 0

Postscript

There is a back-story to this night that I was completely unaware of when it was happening. Initially, I had no idea who this girl was. I was pretty sure I'd never seen her before in my life, which was part of what made these events that much weirder to me. I thought maybe she recognized me from my website—and being that my site hadn't even been up for a year at this point, that was unlikely—or she just thought I was hot. I also thought her friends were trying to keep her away from me because, well, I'm me, and girls should keep their friends away from me.

Wrong.

In reality, it had nothing do with any of those things. It turns out I actually had met the girl before, briefly, while out drinking with some friends one night, and that she had a boyfriend, who her friends were trying to keep her from cheating on. With me. I didn't find this out until the next day when I called Ryan. He told me:

"Dude, you missed the best part. When her friends came to get her the second time, the girl I was talking too said 'I'm going to call her boyfriend, he'll come get her. She's going to do something bad, I just know it.'"

I wondered why she acted so weird the next day. Sobriety brings consequences.

But that's not all. I had some friends in common with her, and I eventually found out that not only did she have a boyfriend, but I knew her boyfriend . . . and her boyfriend HATED me.

You want to guess why she was so eager to fuck me?

Apparently her boyfriend had done something that really pissed her off—I never found out exactly what, but I assume he cheated on her—so when she saw me out she decided to get back at him by fucking me.

I feel so cheap and used!!

FUNNY ODDS AND ENDS

This is a random assortment of small, funny anecdotes that I had left over.

This one girl who emailed me to hook up was obsessed with the idea that most people you meet on the internet are serial killers. I tried to explain that hooking up with me was safer than hooking up with someone she met at a bar. With me, she knew what she was getting into and people could always find me. With some dude at a bar, you don't know anything about him.

She still wanted to meet me in public first, with her friends there, and she would only go back to her place to fuck. Whatever, she was really hot, so I dealt with it. We met out at a bar, and were fucking within the hour.

The whole time, her phone was blowing up with texts from her friends, asking about me, etc. After we were done, she went to the bathroom, so I took her phone, and sent a mass text to her whole address book:

"Help!! LOL!"

Then I turned the phone off, and set it face down on the table. I giggled about this, but didn't really think much more about it, and we got back to fucking some more.

About an hour later, there was loud and urgent pounding on the door. She jumped up, threw a towel over her naked body, and answered it.

It was the cops, with three of her friends.

So yeah, that text message maybe wasn't the best idea.

_____

I hooked up with this girl in LA when I was living there. I went to her place, fucked her, etc, etc. Whereas most people have bookshelves, she had this wall of DVDs—tons and tons of DVDs. Maybe not that strange, except that they were in alphabetical order, and all kinds of ridiculously obscure movie-nerd-type movies. Not the usual DVD wall for a girl. I asked her about them:

Girl "Oh, they're my boyfriend's. He's such a freak about them."
Tucker "You have a boyfriend?"
Girl "Yeah, he's out of town this weekend."

Typical LA girl whore. She went to take a shower, so I took a bunch of the DVDs off the shelves, took the disks out, and put them in the wrong cases. For example, I took the *Raging Bull* DVD and put it into the case for *The Godfather* or something. I did this for about 50 of them, and of course, didn't tell her anything about it.

About a week later, she called me in hysterics.

Girl "DID YOU SWITCH OUT ALL OF HIS DVDS!?!!"
Tucker "Not all of them."
Girl "Thanks, asshole! Now he broke up with me and moved out! This is all your fault!!"
Tucker "Hold on—you cheated on him, and you're blaming me for you breaking up?"

_____

I went to an expensive boarding school that cost more than most colleges and law schools. Middle Eastern sheiks, Russian oligarchs, and

_____

South American land barons sent their kids to this school. The school was dripping in wealth and privilege (not that I had any). And they named ME the most egotistical. That should tell you something.

Biggest Ego?
Tucker Max

The awful picture from my year book

In college, I wasn't named anything. Not because I changed or grew up or whatever, but because I went to the University of Chicago and that is where fun goes to die. We didn't even have a yearbook, let alone a section for superlatives.

Stuck on the south side of Chicago with a bunch of science nerds and no sports teams to follow, I got out of there a year early literally bursting at the seams with untapped collegiate energy. You know how when you haven't jerked off for a while that first next load is a doozy? Yeah, well that was law school. A three-year doozy.

In law school I was named:

1. Most Likely Not to Graduate
2. Most Likely to Spend a Little Time in Jail
3. Most Likely to Be Investigated by a Special Prosecutor
4. Most Likely to Be Convicted of Insider Trading
5. Least Likely to Be an Attorney
6. Most Likely to Be Disbarred
7. Most Likely to Stuff Superlative Ballot Box

And you wonder why they never invite me back for alumni events.

My third year of college, I lived in an apartment off campus, on a street where pretty much all the apartments looked the same. One night I went out—a RARE night at the University of Chicago—and got ridiculously drunk. I noticed as I walked up to my building that the lights were on in my place. I thought I'd turned them off, but I never lock my door, so it was conceivable that a friend had crashed at my place or something.

I opened the door to my apartment, and not only were the lights and TV on, there were like four people sitting in there on my couches watching TV. I had NO IDEA who ANY of these fucking people were. I'd not had a good night out, and I was really drunk, so this was the last straw:

Tucker "GET THE FUCK OUTTA MY APARTMENT!! GET THE FUCK OUTTA MY APARTMENT! RIGHT FUCKING NOW!!!!"

I was seconds from a serious fight—these people had broken into my apartment. Though there were two girls and two guys, in my drunken mind I thought for sure I could take them all. There was some more screaming and pushing involved, and finally one of the dudes gets me to focus enough to realize something:

That wasn't my apartment.

I had walked into the apartment building that was right next to mine. Same building design and layout, same unit, same layout in the apartment, everything the same—except I was one building off.

Whoops.

[My biggest regret was that I wasn't sober or quick enough to drop the classic Doyle Hargraves line from the movie *SlingBlade,* "Get outta my house! That goes for cocksuckers and retards!"]

I was coming back from a bar with a girl, drunk as hell, and I came across this car trying to parallel park. I get behind him and start waving him in, kinda giving directions.

Tucker "OK dude, more to the left, to the left, cut your wheel, come on, plenty of space—"

CRUNCH. He backed right into a light pole and dented the hell out of his bumper.

Tucker "Perfect! Just buff that out, it'll be fine."

As I walked off the guy got out of his car, in complete shock, alternating between staring between me and his car smashed into the light pole, confused as shit. Total dick move, but that's what you get for trusting some random drunk asshole.

———————

SlingBlade and I somehow ended up at some random house party one night in law school. We insisted on talking in redneck voices the entire time. The best part was the people who took us seriously:

Tucker "Hay . . . HAY BUDDY—make this'n thang werk."
Youth "What?"
Tucker [I point to the cover of DVD case I'm holding] "Make this'n here picture show up on that'n thar screen."
Youth "You want me to put the DVD on?"
SlingBlade "MAKE IT WORK!!!"
Youth "You guys are jerks."

———————

An email I sent to my buddies when asked how I deal with dumb girls:

———————

"As per dealing with stupid girls, I use several tactics. One, I act silly. Always cracking ridiculous jokes, being goofy, anything to entertain myself, because this girl is not going to entertain you. Most of the time, the girl is confused at first, but then joins in, and can actually be a little fun herself.

Secondly, I'll ask them something about themselves, something that they like talk a lot about, like their problems, and then do one of two things: completely tune them out and think of other things or I make subtle jokes at their expense, ones that they don't get. Once you make a stupid girl feel comfortable, she'll talk till your ears bleed. At that point, your only concern is what to think of when you're tuning her out. I usually think about how great I am.

If you are going to make fun of them, make sure that you are either way above their head with your jokes, or you do it in a fun way. Dumb girls forgive humor at their expense less easily than smart ones. Also, I'll try the most outrageous thing I can think of. For instance, peeing on the girls in the shower. Or farting during sex. Or asking them to come into the bathroom and hold it for me while I pee. Now, if you are going to take this route, make sure and start small. Make a little burp at dinner. Then pee with the door open. You don't want to alienate her before you get to the good stuff. Once you get her used to you doing these sorts of things, before you know it you'll be plugging her brown hole and using her as a spittoon, all, of course, to be retold in stories to us."

———————

One night I was out in the city with some friends, just a typical night out drinking. I left the bar relatively early to go somewhere else, but my friends stayed behind. After I left, these two random guys came up to them and said:

"Your friend looks like a shorter, fatter version of Tucker Max."

My friends have not let me forget about this since.

———————

———

I'm walking around Chicago one afternoon and I run into a Greenpeace petition drive. For some odd reason Greenpeace decided to use five hot chicks to gather signatures. Devious bastards.

One of the hotties approaches me, and though she is beautiful, I can't resist informing her that I am against her socialist proposal, and counter with a market-based solution. This does not go over well. She calls over a crony who proceeds to engage in a fit of histrionics that would make Gidget blush. She mindlessly spouts off the company line like she's in an infomercial, perhaps due to the fact that she is suffering from the intellectual equivalent of Stockholm Syndrome. I offered to sit her in front of a strobe light to deprogram her, but no dice.

Then, mainly for the comedic value, I ask her if she wants to go to Morton's with me to get a steak. Again, no. She is "against the slaughter of animals." I tell her that I'll overlook the fact that she's wearing leather sandals, if she'll overlook the fact that I like meat. She then informs me that she is "repulsed" by me. I guess that's a little harder to overlook than dietary choices.

———

SlingBlade and I almost got kicked out of a law school final exam because we had been up for like 35 hours and were so punch drunk we could not stop laughing. What were we laughing about? On this site called amithebomb.com there was this pic of two girls bent over standing next to each other, and the caption was 'poon sammich!'

Also, there was another pic of an Asian girl climbing through a window, and it said "You no take Ming arrive!"

He would recite one line and I'd answer with the other . . . for TWO HOURS. Even our friends were pissed at us.

———

One night in law school, all of us were out drinking. Brownhole got really drunk that night. The next day, PWJ told me about their trip home.

Tucker "You have to be kidding! As drunk as he was, he *drove* home last night?"

PWJ "Yeah, it was bad. He did some whippets at the bar, and said he was fine."

Tucker "You're kidding. He lives a hour away."

PWJ "Totally serious. I was drunk enough that I let him drop me off at home. Though I did insist on riding shotgun, so that in case he drove into a pole, I would get the airbag."

———————

I HATE beggars and make it a policy to never give them money. There is a very simple and sound reason for this: Every dollar you give to a beggar is a dollar they don't have to work for. You are essentially paying them to beg. And don't give me that "some people can't work" shit. Even if that is true, you are better off giving your money to a legitimate charity. They are better equipped than you to dispense money in a way that will be effective, as opposed to giving money to some junkie who is a blight on the neighborhood.

That being said, I have given money to a beggar. Once. He was standing on a corner, looking all dopey and dirty, and he simply said,

"Excuse me sir, would you please donate to the United Negro Pizza Fund?"

I laughed out loud and kept walking, then stopped, went back, and gave him two dollars. Why?

He made me laugh, and that has value. If every bum on the street made me laugh, I might change my stance on them. Until that point, they will remain human pigeons to me.

———————

When I was dating HotNurse, one night she asked me for a favor:

HotNurse "Would you go to my hospital's Christmas party with me?"
Tucker "Of course I will."
HotNurse "No, you don't understand. These are the cheesiest, most annoying people ever. You will hate it. If you go, I will owe you big."
Tucker "Come on, how bad can it be?"

Cut to:

This thing was a Christmas abortion. Chinese food and samosas. No beer, only cheap wine. Obnoxious fat girls in Santa hats. The hostess had everyone playing party games. My personal favorite was the one where she passed out 3x5 cards with logos on them, and we had to write down what company each logo belonged to. If we got the most right, we "won." The final straw was Christmas Karaoke.

Tucker "You have to toss my salad tonight."
HotNurse "I know."

My grandfather got a bit senile and out of it before he died:

Pa "Do you have a girlfriend yet?"
Tucker "No."
Pa "What are you, going to be a queer now?"

Ten minutes later:

Pa "So, Tucker, you got a girlfriend?"
Tucker "Nope."
Pa "What are you, sick or something?"

While at the University of Chicago a couple of friends and I went to dinner at some restaurant in China Town night. Oblivious to the fact that my idiocy can be heard outside of a five-foot radius, I started in with the "You been here four hour. You go now," routine. Ha ha, we all laugh because infantile racism is funny.

A little while later I walked back to the bathroom, and as I went down the hall to the "Male Room," I passed this rickety open door. I peered in to see two little Chinese kids looking at me, holding their eyes wide open with their fingers (to give a Caucasian look), and saying:

"Hot Dogs! Baseball! Hot Dogs! Baseball!"

I laughed so hard, I almost didn't make it to the bathroom.

You win this round, Chinese kids.

———

My last trip to Vegas was good. I spent three days drunk off my ass playing blackjack with a former UK player and fucking with all the Carolina alums like Joe Wolf and George Karl by reciting the Dean Smith Prayer. My buddy even had to save my ass from a stomping when I was hammered and asked Desagna Diop if he brought his goats to Vegas.

The highlight was something you couldn't script: A SOBER Larry Eustachy playing blackjack with us, alternately losing $100s a hand and yelling at me because I wasn't drinking fast enough. At one point I had two vodka clubs in front of me and he nearly had an aneurysm:

Eustachy: "Look at that, there is moss on the rim! Are you gonna drink it or just look at it?"
Tucker: "You are the sober one, and you're asking me if I'm gonna drink it? Shit or get off the pot, Bill W."

Eustachy: "Why do you have two if you can't even finish one! Christ, the ice has melted!"

Tucker: "Hey Larry, you wanna go to a frat party?"

The problem is that last night was the very definition of a "had to be there" moment. But I'll try and give an account anyway:

We go to dinner at Gibson's and then across the street to this old school piano bar called Jill's. It's mostly an older crowd but also the kind of place in Chicago where you can have a lot of fun if you know what you are doing. Jill's signature attraction is the electric train that wraps around the entire bar and runs nonstop, open to close. Well we were pretty shitty and my buddy JD decides he wants to touch the train. He waits for it to come by, reaches up to put his hand on it, and of course knocks it off the track. Dexterity is not the domain of the drunkard. JD gets this guilty look on his face, then reaches back up to put the train back on the track.

As he touched the train, something very wrong happened: a shower of sparks started shooting everywhere. All the lights on and around the track flickered, then went off. He immediately pulled his hand away, and I fucking collapsed in laughter.

The bouncer comes running over yelling at him about how he's going to have to pay $1000 for the train. $1000 for a fucking toy train?!? I wouldn't pay $1000 for a REAL one!! Then JD did something that made me nearly shit my pants. With the saddest most pathetic drunk puppy dog eyes I've ever seen, he looks at the bouncer, looks at the train, then looks back at the bouncer and points to some other dude in the bar, as if he is blameless and been wrongly accused.

I couldn't deal with it. I damn near choked I was laughing so hard . . . see, you had to be there.

One night I was at a bar and had an all-around average Tucker night out: excessive drinking, rambunctious behavior, some girls loving us, some girls hating us, and everyone paying attention to us. As we leave, out front is a black Escalade, with Cadillac's new "I have no talent, but I want to be a rapper anyway" option package—chrome 24-inch rims, solid black tinted windows, frog-eye lights, etc.

It is jerking back and forth, and a crowd is gathering around it. Everyone is looking inside, laughing, gawking, and calling to their friends. I walk over as everyone starts chanting, "GO! GO! GO! GO! GO!," and peer inside to see some guy screwing a fat girl donkey style and pointing to the crowd gathered around his Escalade, laughing and having a great old time.

He "finishes" pretty quickly after that, then crawls into the front seat, starts up his SUV, rolls down the window, throws the used condom into crowd, and peels off. I think the condom hit someone in the head.

It's moments like this that make me proud to be human.

———————————

I can't dance. Outside of my six weeks in Cancun, I can count on one hand the number of times I've danced in public. I can count on one FINGER the number of times I've danced with a fat girl.

Credit, Jojo, BrownHole and I were at a bar one night and we saw this group of chubby girls out on the dance floor. We got to talking about how much it would take for us to actually dance with one of them. It quickly became a contest. We each wrote down our minimum price for dancing with a certain fat girl we'd separated from the herd. The low bidder then had to dance with her if the other three agreed to put up the money.

Credit's bid: $300.
Jojo's bid: $250.
BrownHoles's bid: $450.

———————————

My bid: $80.

And to think, I studied Econ in college.

They gladly put up the money. I had to dance with her for two songs and smack her ass. I danced with her for ONE song, whacked her on the ass and then brought her over to talk to Credit. She thought he was cute.

This one ridiculous JAP-y girl I met in Cancun annoyed the fuck out of me. From some Philadelphia suburb I think, really obnoxious voice, she was the type that wanted to fuck me, but didn't want to admit it to herself. She tried to play hard to get by being bitchy, and wasn't emotionally intelligent enough to understand this wasn't working with me. I'll never forget the exchange that finally shut her up. It started with her trying to deny that she was JAP-y (Jewish American Princess), and then went downhill from there:

Tucker "You are the very *definition* of a JAP."
JapGirl "I am not! How am I JAP-y?"
Tucker "OK, let's see . . . what did you tell me earlier about how you fuck?"
JapGirl "Ugh! I just like being on bottom because I'm lazy. I don't like moving. I like the guy to do the work."
Tucker "Yeah, you're not JAP-y at all."
JapGirl "I'm not! I just like to get my way and if I don't I cry until I do."
Tucker "You sound like a joy in bed."
JapGirl "Are you good in bed?"
Tucker "If I cum, that means I was good."
JapGirl "What? No, it doesn't work that way. I want to cum too."
Tucker "Then cum."
JapGirl "You have to make me cum."
Tucker "How long is it going to take for you to figure out that I don't give a flying shit if you cum or not?"
JapGirl "UGH, fine! Well how big is your dick? Maybe if it's big enough, I'll cum anyway."

Tucker "Not big. Just average."

JapGirl "No see, I need a guy with a big dick. You need to have a big dick."

Tucker "Comparing dick sizes is stupid and irrelevant. It's not the size of the dick that matters, it's who goes home with the girl."

JapGirl "Yeah, but the size of the dick is relevant to me, because it determines whether I cum or not. Big dick, good orgasm. Small dick, fake orgasm."

Tucker "You are talking about this like it's supposed to matter to me."

JapGirl "It IS supposed to matter to you. If I have to fake an orgasm with you, that means you're lame."

Tucker "No it doesn't. You are missing the point. If you are faking an orgasm with me, I've already won. Not because you are faking it, but because I fucked you."

———————

One I'm out with Bunny and D-Rock at my new favorite Chicago bar. D-Rock sees a girl he wants to hit on, and of course, I am obligated to talk to her fat friend.

But this was a different fat girl. This fat girl thought she was smart. That is a bad thing for a fat girl to think . . . especially when she is criminally stupid. And around Tucker Max.

She asked me what I did for a living. I told her she wouldn't believe me. She insisted I tell her. I told her I was a diet consultant. She didn't believe me. Then it got bad:

Fat girl "Where did you go to school?"
Tucker "University of Chicago."
Fat girl "What was your degree in?"
Tucker "Econ."
Fat girl "Econ? What can you do with an econ degree?"

At that point, I was laughing so hard I had to walk away. D-Rock just shook his head.

———————

Fat girl "No really, what can you do with an econ degree?"
Tucker "You obviously went to a state school. A BAD state school."
Fat girl "I want to know what you can do with an econ degree."
Tucker "Do you even know what finance is?"
Fat girl "You can't work in finance with an econ degree. You need a finance degree."

God bless her oversized heart. I haven't laughed that hard in months. While I composed myself, D-Rock tried to explain to her that an econ degree from the University of Chicago is one of the top five most marketable degrees, along with engineering/comp sci from MIT and maybe one or two Harvard degrees. And that a finance degree is basically just a watered down econ degree for stupid state school idiots. I finally composed myself and came back for the resolution:

Tucker "Seriously, what state school did you go to?"
Fat girl "Michigan State."
Tucker "HAHHAHAHHAHAHHAHAHAHAHAHHAHHHAHHAHHAHHAHA. I WAS RIGHT!!!!"

Unintentional comedy at its finest. It's not easy to make me laugh that hard.

———————

My buddy Brian and I were walking into a bar when I stopped to take a piss on a tree. These two girls walked by and gave me a sideways glance, then kept walking. About 50 feet down the sidewalk, they turned and asked us to take a picture of them, but instead of handing us a camera they just started talking to us. They were OK-looking, and at least one had some personality, so we went with it and invited them into the bar with us to get drinks.

It was painfully clear after less than a full drink that neither was going to fuck me within the next thirty minutes, which was pretty much the only justification for me speaking to them.

———————

So I got bored. What happens when I get bored talking to marginal girls? Exactly.

I forget specifically what it was that finally crossed the line with one of the girls . . . I think it was when I said that her Chinese character tattoo meant "shameless whore" instead of "hell cat" as she claimed. Or it might have been when they told me they went to Loyola Law School, and I told them they'd have been better off getting their law degree in the mail. Whatever it was that pissed her off, she started castigating me and then it happened:

Girl #1 "You totally blew your chance. There you were peeing on a tree, and these two very hot girls walked in front of you and—"
Girl #2 "What hot girls?"
Girl #1 "US!"
Girl #2 "Oh . . . yeah."
Tucker "HAHAHAHAHAHAHAHAHAHAHAHAH! That was going to be my question too! WHAT HOT GIRLS! HAHAHHAHHAHAHAHAHAHHA! You are the first honest woman I've met in years—God bless you."
Girl #2 had one of those fleeting moments of honesty that are so rare in women. She turned bright red, tried to reverse her position, but it was over.

My night was made.

Tucker debates postmodernism, wrestles midgets

Occurred, December 2002

One Friday I met up with some friends from college, who are all lawyers, and went to a happy hour for some associate who was leaving his firm. We began with the Jungle Fever of liquor combos—tequila and Jaeger shots—and numerous beers later, we went to this incredibly upscale yuppie bar where douchebags with 3-Series order stupid drinks like gimlets. I hate everyone and everything about this place.

Most of the people leave, so it's me, my friend Jim, his girlfriend, two female associates from his firm, and a male associate. It comes out that Jim, his girlfriend, and I are going to midget boxing on Saturday night. This is a very abbreviated version of what followed:

The girls go ballistic.

They launch into all sorts of ridiculous histrionics about what horrible people we must be to exploit midgets in this way. Exploit? Yeah bitch, if everyone stops going to midget boxing, these midgets will suddenly become neurosurgeons. And tall. Bullshit—they just become unemployed. Plus, they're adults, and we should treat them like adults. Tiny, little adults. If you're a midget, and you want to box, you pretty much have to either become a midget boxer or just fight children in alleys; you're not going toe-to-toe with Mike Tyson.

They respond with lots of fancy, meaningless words like "exploitation" and "commodification." They also tell me I need to read some Catherine MacKinnon, some Andrea Dworkin, and perhaps even some Michel Foucault. Saying those names to me, you might as well set off a bomb in the bar.

I tried for a good ten minutes to let it go, I really did, but with Red Bull and vodka coursing through my veins, and the names of the intellectual antichrists being thrown around so flippantly, I let loose. Absolutely unleashed. I eventually started throwing out words like "fascist" and "not content to let people live their own lives" and "if you don't like stumpy people hitting each other, don't go see it" and "these theories only sound good or important to upper-middle-class-usually-white-people who feel guilty about their status, and have taken enough benefits out of capitalism that they have the luxury of enough leisure time to actually think about this crap and go to $35K/year schools to learn it."

Then it got ugly. Sort of like her face.

Bitch "This persona you take on seems to be a very direct product of this culture and the construction of masculinity within this culture. You've done an impressive job with it."
Tucker "Aren't you just the cutest postmodern social constructionist I've ever seen!! Funny how masculinity is 'constructed' in just about the same way in every culture . . . hmmm, I smell something . . . not teen spirit . . . smells like a common cause . . . human nature maybe?"

We went back and forth pitting our diametrically opposed ideologies against each other on various battlegrounds, until I pull out the trump card and point out the obvious: that they were attorneys at very large Chicago firms, and if they really thought "commodification" and "exploitation" were meaningful concepts, perhaps they should look for other lines of work, and "stop being preposterous hypocrites who are milking the tit of the cow they were trying to slaughter." This last comment hit home. The male associate (who was on my side) quickly grabbed the check before blood was spilled.

So of course, on Saturday I go to the midget boxing with Jim and his wife. The only people exploited are us.

It opens with a dwarf named, I shit you not, "Puppet the Psycho Dwarf." He was the foulest dwarf in all of Middle Earth and he gets up on stage and starts shouting "WHO WANTS TO SEE A MIDGET BLEEEEEED TONIGHT!?!!!" into the microphone. Repeatedly. There are differences between dwarves and midgets, by the way. I didn't know this at first, but the difference is that dwarves all live together and work in diamond mines, and midgets all punch each other in the face for money.

After getting everybody ramped up, this dwarf then goes on an un-stoppable ten-minute rant. He's pointing at girls in the audience, telling them that he could smell their pussies when he walked by, and talking about when he has them doggie-style he'll have extra leverage because he'll be standing, not on his knees. He's bragging about his 12-inch inseam and how, when he gets it up, he can pole vault down the street. The girls are going nuts, loving it. I mean, what's more of a turn-on to a woman than vulgar sex-talk from someone you'll never in a million years wake up next to? One girl was so into it, she was offering to suck his dick at the top of her lungs. It was crazy. And it stopped there.

The whole thing turns out to be midget WWF. All fake. Poorly acted. I paid ten dollars to see it, and I desperately want it back. And of course, the fucking midgets are laughing all the way to their tiny little piggy banks.

The highlight came when this normal-sized guy—we'll call him "human" for short—got into the ring (part of the act), and they accused him of wanting to be a midget. He protested in that overly-expressive way they do on "Monday Night Raw" so the poor people in the rafters can see, and then three of the midgets beat the crap out of him. It would have been funny if it weren't so unfair. You can't one-and-a-half-team a dude like that.

This was nearly tolerable. Nearly. Then it got weird. Two *other* "humans" got in the ring and started rapping. They weren't black. They weren't midgets. They weren't even good at rapping. They were just two white guys in a wrestling ring, yelling unmelodic stupidity into microphones. We left.

THE DBA STORY

During the spring semester of my first year of law school there was an election at Duke Law School for the Duke Bar Association (DBA). The DBA is essentially the law school student government, and like all governments everywhere, it is an ineffectual, worthless organization filled with small-minded, sanctimonious, self-important twits who want to exercise power without having to actually do something to earn it.

I was sitting in the library, bored out of my mind, and came upon a flyer promoting the DBA election. It was ridiculously self-important and pretentious, but more importantly, it explained that the candidate statements would be posted on a bulletin board in the middle of the law school, along with a picture of the candidate.

So here I was, with an opportunity to not only fuck with pretentious shits, but with a chance to write insane nonsense and then have it posted next to the pictures of my friends. You don't have to ask me twice.

These are the candidate statements I wrote for myself and my friends:

Tucker Max:

My name is Tucker Max and I am applying for a position on the Graduate and Professional Student Council.

If elected, I promise to go to the Graduate and Professional Student Council meetings very drunk and demand to vote on things not on the agenda. Then I will take my shirt off so everyone can look at my rippling muscles. And possibly even my pants, but only if I have on boxer-briefs under them.

If I am still not getting my way, I will drag a dead, rotting deer carcass into the meeting, bellowing, "I AM NOW YOUR KING!! FLEE BEFORE MY WRATH!!" Then I will unleash my thundering horde upon the dissenters, until all my enemies are driven before me and crushed under my Cole-Haan loafers.

Once I gain control of the Graduate and Professional Student Council, I will declare myself ruler for life. My first decree will be that all grad student basketball tickets go to law students and hot girls who like me. I will then appoint someone Distributor of The Tickets, who will oversee the distribution of the tickets and the seating arrangements. That person could be you if you vote for me.

Then I will annex the University and its land, and declare a free state. And open a liquor store, with real cheap prices.

Respectfully submitted,
Tucker Max

Hate:

I am Hate. I WILL be your next Class Representative.

Why am I qualified? The obvious reason is because I said so. My other skills include: pointing out the obvious things that everyone misses, darts, ruling over committee meetings with an iron fist, and critiquing the obvious flaws in poorly made movies.

Why should you vote for me? Do you enjoy your teeth?

My motto is simple: "Just because I don't like you, doesn't mean that you can't vote for me."

Hate, Class of 2001

GoldenBoy:

My name is GoldenBoy, and I would like to be your Library Committee Representative.

I feel that I am qualified for this position because I am very well read, I like libraries, and most importantly I am smarter than you are. With my superior intellect, I feel that I could do something for the Library Committee that has never been done before. What that is, I am not sure, but that doesn't change the fact that I am very smart, which you would know if you have ever had a class with me.

If elected, my first action will be to look down on you from my perch of enlightenment. My second action will be to sneer at you, as you look up at me from your little hovels of ignorance. My third action will be to talk as much as possible in all my classes.

Sincerely,
GoldenBoy-The People's Candidate
Class of 2001

El Bingeroso:

My name is El Bingeroso. I am running for Faculty Appointments Committee Representative. My platform can be summarized by a silly little ballad I wrote during Criminal Law:

I am pretty, oh so pretty!
Everybody, oh everybody,
Please come look at me!
I am pretty, oh so pretty!
I want to appoint all the Faculty!
If I win, I'll sing this song in front of everyone.

Your Friend,
El Bingeroso, Class of 2001

Credit:

My name is Credit, and I am running for the Appeals Board.

I think I would make a good candidate because I am very appealing, hey! Also, I would add spice to the meetings by saying things like, "Lets'a go!" and "Who here ordered dis here pizza," even if there ain't no pizzas around.

Doin' it for da kids,
Credit

JoJo:

My name is JoJo, and I would like to be your DBA Class Representative. You might have seen me around, I'm that black guy. The one with that thing on his face.

If I was like everyone else, I would promise you a bunch of ridiculous crap that I couldn't deliver on. But I'm not going to. Why? Because I am cooler than Shaft. I am more super than SuperFly. I AM THE BLACK CAESAR!

To me this election is about diversity, and it doesn't get more diverse than me. I am African, African-American, American, and Native American. And don't forget that I'm cool as Miles Davis.

I will make you one promise if you elect me. I will coolify this law school. I'll show all the silly Bitterman look-a-likes how to dress, act, and just be an overall pimp. And I won't sell out in the process, like Damon Wayans.

I also want to bring some life to the DBA. If elected, I will grow an Angela Davis- looking afro. Then, I will free the law school from 400 years of oppression. Then I will change my name to Mandingo Dele.

Keepin' it real,
JoJo, Esquire To Be
Class of 2001

———————

Well, little did I realize what would happen. The DBA lost its collective shit. The person in charge of the election, David Dixon, went nuts. How nuts? Read the story in the Duke Law newspaper:

Practical Joker Blows up Chances at Election

by Barbara Goffman

The gag was on a practical joker last week, who was barred from running in the DBA election because of a prank he pulled.

DBA Vice President Dave Dixon blocked 1L Tucker Max from running in Thursday's election after Max impersonated four 1Ls. Max had entered the election himself, seeking to be a representative to the Graduate and Professional Student Council (GPSC). Max also had submitted fake statements of intent to run in the election, as well as facetious platforms, under the names of four friends.

———————

"I thought it was funny," Max said Tuesday night of the stunt. "This process begs for this sort of thing."

But Dixon, who organized the election, was not amused.

"I agree at some level that they were funny," Dixon said. "People have submitted flippant statements before. But submitting statements in someone else's name is what I have a problem with."

DBA President Andrew Flake agreed, saying that Max's action "mocks the whole electoral process."

Dixon discovered the prank accidentally. He sent out emails to all the students who had entered the election, reminding them of the deadline for submitting their platforms. Two people wrote back, saying they had never thrown their names in the ring. About the same time, other students told Dixon about the stunt and Max's role in it.

Dixon confronted Max, who admitted his actions. Dixon then disqualified Max from running in the election and reported the incident to Susan Sockwell, associate dean for student affairs.

"I felt I was required to report it because it was close enough to an honor code violation," Dixon said.

Other DBA board members agreed. During a discussion of the incident at Tuesday's weekly DBA meeting, 3L Representative Kim Lerman remarked that Max's actions have "got to be an honor code violation."

Yet they aren't, Sockwell said. The code only covers specific listed offenses, such as plagiarism or use of unauthorized materials on an exam.

"I do not see that his submissions of fake, practical-joke election statements is a violation of one of the listed offenses in our honor code,"

Sockwell said Wednesday. "I told Tucker that I think it is misconduct but not an honor code violation, and he will not be prosecuted under the honor code."

Max is not necessarily off the hook, however. The preamble to the honor code allows the administration or faculty to separately address all other types of student misconduct, Sockwell said.

"There are other avenues to deal with misconduct. I'm still considering that. I don't know what I'm going to do," she said.

Max, meanwhile, had challenged his election disqualification. "My Statement of Intent was submitted in accordance with every rule that I could find," Max wrote in an email to Dixon on Feb. 24. "I submitted it with the full intention of running, and . . . I expect to be given the same considerations as every other person who ran."

Dixon maintained his action was permissible. The DBA Constitution says that the vice president may promulgate reasonable election rules and regulations, Dixon pointed out. The DBA board backed Dixon unanimously in a vote of confidence Tuesday.

After learning that his bid was rejected, Max said this whole incident had become "comical."

"I wouldn't have done this to someone I thought would have a remote chance of being offended," Max said. "I honestly figured someone would read these [platforms] and recognize immediately that they were fake. The whole thing should have taken five minutes at the most."

But Dixon ended up spending far more time on this issue. Between investigating the fake nominations, rewriting the ballots, and discussing the problem with Sockwell and the DBA board, Dixon said he wasted about 10 hours.

"I thought it was possibly defamatory to have these statements attributed to these people," Dixon said. "At the beginning, I had no idea if these were people [whom Max] hated."

———————

So after the DBA decided to fuck with me and not allow any of the candidates to run OR put the candidates' statements up on the board, did I stand by and do nothing? Well, yeah, pretty much. Honestly, I thought the whole thing was too absurd to waste my time on, even though my time was completely worthless. I did write a response though:

"Keeping with the 'any press is good press' maxim, I have written a response to the article in the last *Duke Law Reporter* about my role in the recent election fiasco. In case you have forgotten the whole election fiasco over break (as you should have), I'll refresh your memory. I wrote five statements of intent to run in the recent DBA election, four of which were for people not named Tucker Max. The statements themselves were (admittedly) submitted as jokes, were totally inoffensive, and were in the names of four of my close friends, none of whom are at all upset at me for any of this.

I'd like to begin by correcting some glaring errors in the article. First of all, David Dixon NEVER 'confronted me.' I still have no idea what this guy looks like. I would make guesses, but I won't because they'd probably all be libelous.

Second, I was not really 'denied an opportunity to run.' All the statements, including my own, were submitted as jokes. I initially had no intention of running, and neither did anyone else. In reality, I just wanted to see these absurd statements on a poster board with my friends' pictures next to them. Once I realized that I was running for an uncontested spot, and Dixon asked me if I really wanted to run, I told Dixon (in an email) that I would fill the position. This was obviously before he had his fit of indignant rage, and decided to disqualify me and my friends.

———————

Enough with the clarifications, on with the rant. My favorite part of the article was where Andrew Flake said that I made a mockery of the 'whole election process.' Is he kidding? That's like saying that Jimmy Swaggart made a mockery of televangelism. As if the DBA were this bastion of respectability and icon of professionalism until I came along and ruined everything. Insolent Tucker Max has forever sullied the lustrous reputation of the DBA. How will the law school ever recover? Who will govern us? Who will lead?

A delicious irony in this absurd comedy is the fact that of the three people who elected to stay in the race after the statements were discovered as jokes, two were running for UNCONTESTED SPOTS. This means that we were disqualified for positions that no one else wanted. Apparently the DBA would rather have the spots unfilled than have someone with a sense of humor occupy them.

One of my favorite acts in this little drama was an email that David Dixon was kind enough to send me, in which he urged me to 'engage in some serious thought about the fact that you are in a professional school, not a junior high school,' and went on to hope that 'this experience in law school will help redirect your paths toward the standard of professional conduct that absolutely will be required of you in your chosen vocation.'

Thanks, Dave! Boy, if that little bit of sage wisdom didn't turn my life around. I'll start down this path by writing some tax legislation, maybe that'll make me professional! Or even better yet, I'll become a humorless automaton and rigidly enforce meaningless, bureaucratic rules!

I am having trouble figuring out why this whole thing upset people. The statements were not offensive, and the people whose names they were in found them funny. What does it say when David is more upset than the people whose names were used without consent? If I had written something like, 'If elected, I promise to kill all the [insert favorite racial/ethnic group],' then the indignant lather that David and his little henchpeople got worked up into would be rightly justifiable. But not only were the statements not at all offensive to anyone, but the people that they were about thought that they were funny.

I also can't figure out why the actual statements of intent themselves were never printed. My guess is that either the newspaper didn't have a copy of them (coincidentally, they never asked me for copies), or the DBA didn't want them printed, because then those of us free of major head injury would realize how ridiculous this whole situation has become.

Some other things I was surprised that didn't make it into the *Duke Law Reporter* article: a more in-depth examination of David Dixon's basically unchecked power over the DBA elections, how David Dixon threatened (never to my face, of course) my law school career, how incredibly funny the actual statements were, and why none of the quotes from the interviews of those the statements were about made it into the article.

The lesson to be learned from this whole fiasco is . . . don't go to law school. Well, not really. The real lesson is probably something about restraint and maturity, but I never learn those lessons."

The really ironic thing is that the editor of the *Duke Law Reporter,* Alyssa Rubensdorf, wouldn't print my response. Why? SHE THOUGHT IT MIGHT BE LIBELOUS! I swear to God she said that. What a moron. Whatever. That is why all those losers are now miserable lawyers who hate their lives, and I'm Tucker Max.

HOMELESS PEOPLE ARE GOOD FOR SOMETHING

Occurred, July 2006

So today I am eating breakfast at Phillipe's, a famous spot in LA. I go to the bathroom to piss, and all the urinals are occupied so I have to use a stall. As I am pissing someone calls me and instead of just waiting till I was done like a normal person, I fumble through my pockets for my cell . . . and drop my car keys right into the toilet bowl.

I stood there for a good ten seconds contemplating what the fuck I had done. Not only was my piss in the bowl, the water was yellow when I got there . . . and there were shit marks on the side of the bowl.

FUCK.

I momentarily contemplated just ditching them and buying a new car. Seriously. I am not putting my hand in there. There are some battles you just don't want to win, let alone fight. Unfortunately, even though I am doing well financially, I'm not doing THAT well. So what the fuck do I do now? Then it popped into my head:

I went a block away to where I had seen a bunch of homeless people hanging out (LA is crawling with disgusting vagrants) and walked up to a group of them:

Tucker "Any of you want to make ten dollars? All you have to do is get my keys out of the toilet at Phillipe's."

They kinda stood there staring at me for a minute, then one of them agreed and followed me to the bathroom. When he saw the toilet, he paused and said, "Do you have the money?" I produced the cash and without missing a beat he reached into the yellowish brown water and fished them out like a trout from a mountain spring. Then he crossed the line. He tried to fucking hand them to me:

Tucker "What the fuck?!? Put them in the sink."

He placed them under the faucet, I gave him the money and he left. WITHOUT WASHING HIS HANDS. Then I let the water run over them for five minutes, got a cup of bleach from the busboy, and let them soak while I ate.

This was literally the only time in my life I have ever been happy that homeless people exist.

Boyfriend copies Tucker

Judging by the emails I get, there are a lot of guys out there pretending to be me. Not just acting like me mind you: These guys are at bars telling girls that their name is Tucker Max, and pretending that they *actually are me.*

I don't really have any cool stories about busting a guy doing this in the moment—I wish, because that would be fucking awesome—but I do get emails about it all the time. Three of my favorites:

Not All Imitation Is Flattering

Occurred, May 2007

This was one of the first ones I ever got like this:

> From: [name redacted]
> To: Tucker Max <tuckermax@gmail.com>
> Date: May 12, 2007
> Subject: Pissed off
>
> I am perturbed. I recently discovered your site and have been reading some of your stories, because obviously that is the best method of preparation for a criminal procedure exam tomorrow, and I am becoming increasingly paranoid. I will explain:

I recently dated and broke up with a smart, funny, success- ful guy, who in his past (since he met me, to a lesser extent) made a habit of being the drunkest person in the bar (some- times the drunkest person EVER to have been in the bar) and saying and doing ridiculously offensive things. He wooed me with his wit, for the most part, along with his embracing being an asshole (not to me of course), loving attention as I do, and asserting that he is smarter than other people.

Back to where you come in: I am relaying this to you, the author of your site, the only person with a real grip on how unusual your thoughts/actions/expressions are . . .

- he consistently says, if they can't take a joke, fuck 'em

- favorite words = Open Bar

- favorite book = *Confederacy of Dunces*

- uses term "*HIS NAME* drunk"

- tells a story about thinking he was doing "cheers" with himself in a mirror

- his epic story is about having anal sex with a girl while his friend is filming her in the closet . . .

I could go on. So . . . how old is your site? Is this coincidence? Are there a lot of guys out there with similar worldviews?

I can't bear the thought that I was duped by someone copying someone else's shtick. Insights and confidence appreciated.

I broke the news to her that my website had—at that point—been up five years and I already had a bestselling book out. She got pissed, and so I offered her the best way possible to get back at him. Fuck the real Tucker Max.

So she flew to my city and did just that. Then sent her ex a picture of us in bed with the caption:

"He doesn't have to fake it, and for once neither did I."

Ouch.

So What Gave It Away?

Occurred, April 2010

Another email from a different girl I kinda want to know how she "found out" it wasn't me:

"I wanted to tell you that I'm a huge fan. You may be an asshole but I respect that . . . plus you're sexy and you make me laugh. But not that long ago I was out at a bar in Pittsburgh with some friends and this guy approached me and introduced himself as Tucker Max and said he was in town on a book signing. HE LOOKED EXACTLY LIKE YOU! He was even an asshole like you. I really thought he was you. Long story short, I slept with this guy and later found out it was not you. His name is John and he is a student at University of Pittsburgh. This guy gets tons of pussy in Pittsburgh because he tells people he's you. I wish it had been :("

SOMETIMES THE TRUTH DOES HURT

Occurred, July 2008

This exchange disturbed even me. The thing that makes me laugh the most is how, the angrier she gets, the BETTER her spelling and grammar get. Usually works the other way around:

> From: [name redacted]
> To: Tucker Max <tuckermax@gmail.com>
> Date: July 20, 2008
> Subject: lets do that again
>
> omg ur email is so on ur site liar, i knew it was im emailing u instead of txt my phone is annying . . . . u have my number call me today lets get togethr again that was awesum. i believe all ur sotries now that i met u, u are so fun . . . :)

> From: Tucker Max <tuckermax@gmail.com>
> To: [name redacted]
> Date: July 20, 2008
> Subject: re: lets do that again
>
> I honestly don't know what you are talking about. I was alone last night.

From: [name redacted]
To: Tucker Max <tuckermax@gmail.com>
Date: July 20, 2008
Subject: lets do that again

haha, me too, i was alone with ur cock in me . . . seriously cum over, i am soooo horny right nowww ;)

From: Tucker Max <tuckermax@gmail.com>
To: [name redacted]
Date: July 20, 2008
Subject: re: lets do that again

I don't know if youre kidding or not, but I am in Shreveport, Louisiana filming a movie, and I was alone last night. And the night before. I haven't fucked for like four days. If you don't believe me, check the movie site: www.ihopetheyservebeerinhell.com

From: [name redacted]
To: Tucker Max <tuckermax@gmail.com>
Date: July 20, 2008
Subject: lets do that again

omg. is this a joke? stop it. U werent in calgary last night???

From: Tucker Max <tuckermax@gmail.com>
To: [name redacted]
Date: July 20, 2008
Subject: re: lets do that again

Are you fucking stupid? Why would I EVER be in Calgary?

From: [name redacted]
To: Tucker Max <tuckermax@gmail.com>
Date: July 20, 2008
Subject: lets do that again

WHAT!?! THEN WHO DID I SLEEP WITH???

From: Tucker Max <tuckermax@gmail.com>
To: [name redacted]
Date: July 20, 2008
Subject: re: lets do that again

You have be kidding me. I hope you are just fucking with me to get a response.

From: [name redacted]
To: Tucker Max <tuckermax@gmail.com>
Date: July 20, 2008
Subject: lets do that again

NO! I HAD SEX WITH A GUY WHO CLAIMED HE WAS YOU! HE TOLD ALL YOUR STORIES AND LOOKED LIKE U! r u sure you werent in calgary . . . or maybe your cousin or some brother or something?

From: Tucker Max <tuckermax@gmail.com>
To: [name redacted]
Date: July 20, 2008
Subject: re: lets do that again

AHHAHAHAHAHA-only a Canadian girl.
I would tell you that if you want the real thing you can come down to Shreveport and fuck me, but I don't really want to follow some cross-eyed Molson swilling yokel into the same pussy.

From: [name redacted]
To: Tucker Max <tuckermax@gmail.com>
Date: July 20, 2008
Subject: lets do that again

FUCK U . . . HE LOOKED JUST LIKE U! omg. omg. no wonder he told me not ot email him to call hium instead! omg, i let him cum on my face!

I had to stop emailing her at that point. This was too much, even for me.

Ladies, if you are ever out and some guy tells you that he is Tucker Max, there is a very simple test to verify that: Ask to see his ID. I will ALWAYS be willing to show you my driver's license, and then you can know you are fucking/hating the real me.

I do realize that it's possible to make fake IDs, but if a guy wants to go the trouble of making a fake ID just to be able to fuck girls using my name . . . I almost think he deserves it. That is way too much work.

THE TIME I GOT ARRESTED
AT O'HARE AIRPORT

Occurred, June 1996

It is the last day of my freshman year in college, and my dorm is having a huge party. Well, sort of. About ten of us, pretty much the only ones left after finals, are getting really drunk because we are all leaving for the summer the next day, and we want to drink all the alcohol we have left in our respective mini-fridges.

Like most college dorms, the liquor that is left at the end of the year is an odd menagerie of the drinkable, the tolerable, and the barely even potable. We started by drinking normal drinks, like Absolut and cranberry. We ended up finishing with unspeakable concoctions: Triple Sec and E & J. Triple Sec was too sweet for one kid so he stuck with something more conventional—sweet vermouth. Straight. Try that one time; see if you can finish a sip without wanting to set your tongue on fire.

Of course the night descends into inebriated debauchery, replete with everything that happens when 18-, 19-, and 20-year-olds get drunk: people throw up, furniture gets broken, food gets thrown everywhere, more people throw up, urination occurs in inappropriate places (closet, empty mini-fridge), people hook up who would ordinarily not even talk to each other when they are sober. By the time we were finished, our dorm looked like a tornado had blown through a Wal-Mart.

At about 4am, I decide that there is no reason for me to sleep, because I have a 2pm flight out of O'Hare. So I continue to drink, with reckless abandon, and continue the standard Tucker Max drunk act (e.g., urinating on inappropriate surfaces). At about 7am, after everyone else is either passed out or knocked out, I decide to head for the airport, figuring I'll sober up there.

I make it to O'Hare Airport at 8am. The airport is just beginning to come alive, and the ridiculously long lines for everything at O'Hare won't begin for another hour or so. I check my three bags at the curb and proceed directly to security. My body is craving coffee and food and death. I get to the checkpoint, place my backpack and my carry-on on the conveyor belt, and walk through the metal detector.

I stand there, drunker than Hemingway, waiting for my bags to come out, not noticing the conveyor belt had stopped and the federal rent-a-cops were all tripping over themselves, frantically running around. I was occupied with this really hot girl walking by, trying to think of a way to get her attention. Little did I know.

That's when I felt the first of what would be many violent blows to my skull. A large, angry Chicago policeman had given me a forearm shiver from behind, and was on top of me, beating me like I was Rodney King. As if this force weren't enough to restrain a drunk 170-pound college freshman, three to five other CPD joined in the fun, all of them venting every bit of their working class, ugly wife-having frustration upon my drunk, pronated body. Then the group of them picked me up and began dragging me through this maze of doors and tunnels leading into the bowels of O'Hare airport. I'm pretty sure this is how Jimmy Hoffa disappeared.

It was at that point I started to cry.

You have to remember, in a matter of eight seconds, I went from drunk, erotic fantasies of me doing naughty things with an anonymous hot girl, to having my head driven into a marble floor and the shit kicked out of me in front of hundreds of people. For no reason I could discern. So I start bawling. Crying like Jimmy Swaggart. It was a complete joke.

The only thing I can think of, being drunk and not yet 21, is that I had a bottle of half-full Ron Llave rum in my backpack (don't ask me what I was going to do with it). So I start yelling, "It's just rum!! It's just rum!! For the love of God, why are you doing this??" I was scared shitless, bleeding, in serious pain, with no idea what the fuck was going on.

Ignoring my lamentations, and without saying a word, the cops tossed me into a holding cell somewhere deep inside the airport and far away from passengers who could hear my screams. They put me into what amounted to a broom closet with bars, and told me to shut up. Of course, that advice didn't work. The adrenaline had at this point kicked my drunkenness, and I was pissed.

Why the fuck was this happening? I was screaming like a banshee until one of the cops finally told me why I had been detained—I HAD A PISTOL IN MY BACKPACK! Ohhhhhhhh, riiiiggghttt, the pistol. WTF?!?! Who did he think I was, Terry Cummings?! Then it hit me. Had I not been bleeding and in a jail, I would have laughed. Here's the deal:

Two months earlier, I was helping a friend of mine clean out his basement, and we found a starter pistol. It looked, felt, and weighed the same as any other .38, except that it only shot blanks. He gave it to me, and I stuck in one of the numerous mini-compartments on my backpack, and never thought about it again.

As I am contemplating the delicious ironies of life, they bring in my luggage and begin to go through it, unpacking and hurling everything I brought until it's all strewn about the floor of this quasi-holding pen.

So I begin to cry. Again. A few minutes later I stop. I start to yell. Then I get angry. Then I cry again. Then I beg them to use their brains. Then I cry again.

At this point, they begin to put things together. I am a white, 18-year-old college student, with nothing except a starter pistol in his backpack, who has broken down in tears multiple times since he was apprehended. Does this sound like a standard terrorist profile to you?

They interviewed me three times in the next four hours, each time asking me the most moronic questions imaginable.

"Are you a terrorist?"
"Who else were you working for?"
"Are any of your relatives Arab?"

I'm serious. About noon, after I had spent much of the previous four hours crying, yelling, sobbing, and even fainting once (I maintain it was from low blood sugar), they realized what had happened. So they told me I could go.

Of course, this was before I saw that all my clothes were still on the floor, and I was the one who got to pick them up, and repack them. And the kicker: as I left the room, one of the cops HANDED ME THE STARTER PISTOL!

Cop "Here, we can't keep this; you take it."

So I had to go pack it in a separate box and check it through to my final destination. They wouldn't even let me throw it away.

Unbelievable.

I've gathered from people well-versed in airport security since that time, that these "police" violated several FAA rules when they let me go. Supposedly, I am required to be booked and arraigned, etc., etc. You have to remember, this was LONG before 9/11. Had this happened post-9/11, no doubt I'd still be in jail. That time, I think maybe my tears got the best of procedure in this case.

Whatever the case, I ended up just barely making my 2pm flight.

MY REAL LIFE LAW SCHOOL APPLICATION ESSAY

Occurred, March 1997

I submitted the essay below as my personal statement in all my law school applications. Verbatim, exactly as you read it on this page. In fact, it's this essay that the admissions committee at Duke Law School read, and then decided it made sense to give me an academic scholarship to their institution:

"I'll never forget the day I decided that I wanted to go to law school.

It was a bitterly cold March day in Chicago, the kind that freezes the mucous all the way up in your sinus cavity. It was finals week, and myself and three friends were studying in the University of Chicago D'Angelo Law library. We would often go there to study because the tunnel connecting the two buildings would allow us to avoid going out in the cold. I was a freshman at the time, and was nearing the end of my first college semester. Calling that semester 'eventful' would be like saying Bob Marley is into marijuana.

Winter in Chicago is depressing. The sun disappears around mid-December, and doesn't reappear until May. The average day is so cold and windy that Chilly Willy would get frostbite. On top of the great weather, I had nothing go right for me that quarter. My winter highlights included being blown down by wind several times (that season saw gusts up to 60mph); falling down in the bathroom and getting a concussion because someone had left the window open and water on the floor had conveniently turned to ice; getting my first collegiate C because I was literally snowed in my dorm one morning and got to the midterm late; and spraining my ankle so bad I couldn't play basketball for two months.

Francis, Mark, Mohan and myself were sitting in the law library, trying to learn Cicero or whoever it was when all of the sudden, Francis looked up with a gleam in his eye that would have made Jack Nicholson proud, and said in his thick Wisconsin accent, "Hey guys . . . let's get naked."

It is probably not in my best interest to repeat verbatim my first response to that statement, but let's just say I expressed confusion and indignation.

Francis explained, "No you idiot; let's streak the law school."

Streak the law school. That was an idea.

Before I knew it, my three friends and I were standing in the bathroom on the sixth floor, butt-naked, planning our strategy (although, due to the cold floor, we did all have our shoes on. That was quite a site; four guys, completely naked, except for their socks and sneakers). We were going to run down the stairs until we got to the second floor, which was the main student study room. That night there were probably up to two hundred students on the floor. Once there, we would circle the room once, and then take the main staircase down to the first floor, where we would sprint through the Green Lounge, into the tunnel that connected our dorm to the law library and back to our rooms.

It was a great plan. I was confident, naked, and ready to expose myself.

Yet, as I prepared to open the door of the bathroom and lay myself bare to everyone in the law school, I didn't realize I had a fifth member of my group. An uninvited, unwelcome guest, who would follow me throughout my disrobed escapade. Murphy, of Murphy's Law fame, was along for the ride, and would make himself known very soon.

I had been chosen to go first (I wonder why?). I steadied myself, took a deep breath, and heaved the bathroom door open to find Mr. Murphy waiting for me. There was, I'm not kidding, a group of female professors standing and chatting in the hallway. It was that exact moment when I realized that not only was I naked, but people were going to see me naked, and not just people, but older women. Had my friends not pushed me from behind, I probably would have just stood there for about a week. It didn't help that one of the professors started giggling.

Once we were in the stairwell, things got better. You might be surprised what lengths people will go to get out of the way of naked college undergraduates. Someone would later describe it as, "like being in a Francis Bacon painting." I'm still not exactly sure how to take that. Yet, once we hit the second floor, Murphy made his presence known, in an excruciatingly painful manner.

As I opened the door from the stairwell to the second floor, I ran full speed into a girl trying to come in the door that I was exiting. The next second and half are still somewhat fuzzy to me, but I remember her falling down, me falling on her, and her water-bottle somehow being shoved directly into my solar plexus.

That HURT.

Somehow I stumbled up, praying that she wouldn't find out my name and charge me with sexual assault, and began sprinting around the room. I looked like Cramer on amphetamines. I had just had an Evian bottle rammed into one of my nerve centers, was disoriented, short of breath, and pulsing with adrenaline, not to mention naked, in front of a lot of people.

As we made it around the room, a surprisingly warm reaction followed. Whistles, clapping, laughter, cat calls, and cheers rang out. Someone actually even complimented our, uh . . . personages. My ex-girlfriend thinks they were being facetious.

With things now running somewhat smoothly, we exited the second floor, leaving the stressed-out law students with something to laugh about, and headed down the main stairway to the first floor. Coming down the stairs, the order had gotten mixed, and Mohan was now in front, with me second and the other two pulling up the, uh, rear. At the bottom of the main stairway, one can turn right to go out the front door, or turn left to go through the Green lounge and into the tunnel that leads to our dorm. Next to the front door sits the night security guard, who does nothing other than check bags and ID's.

When we came within sight of the night security guard, I honestly thought he was going to combust. His eyes got the size of softballs and popped out of their sockets, every vein on his head bulged to the point of hemorrhage, he shot up out of his chair like a pound of C-4 was detonated beneath him, and screamed as if his toupee was ablaze. Mohan stalled at the bottom of the staircase, not understanding why he would be so upset. Running naked through the law school may not be administration endorsed, but it definitely is not a reason to risk aneurysm.

Mohan and I turned to go into the Green lounge, found Mr. Murphy hanging out in there, and immediately realized why the security guard was so upset.

Of all the nights we could have picked to streak the law school, we had chosen a night that there was a reception for about a hundred people. We later found out that it was a cocktail party for assorted dignitaries from several different law schools, and was considered a very important function.

At this point, there was to be no turning back, literally. With the security guard and his arthritic knees chasing us through the thirty-yard long Green lounge, the four of us did our best head-down-in-a-dead-sprint to the door at the other end. By the time we made it to the doors, you could have heard a mouse fart in that room. EVERYONE had stopped what they were doing and watched this almost tragic comedy unfold. Four naked boys were running through the reception, with a decrepit guard limping after them as if they had stolen the Queen's jewels.

Now, right now you might be asking, why would this possibly make someone want to go to law school? I was pretty sure I wanted to go to law school before that incident. Actually, I'm not really sure why that sealed it for me. My ex-girlfriend thinks that I just can't wait to go back to a place where people would applaud me naked. In all probability, I just thought I could recycle this story to make some more law school people laugh, while at the same time helping my chances of admission to [insert law school here]."

SPECIAL BONUS

More SlingBlade Stuff

People are always pestering me for more SlingBlade material, so here are some emails he sent me reviewing movies he'd just seen.

The Hulk

TOO MUCH TALK MAKE SLINGBLADE ANGRY. SLINGBLADE SPOT PLOT HOLES LARGER THAN WHORES' USED UP VAGINA. SLINGBLADE WANT TO SMASH PUNY HUMANS WHO MAKE HULK MOVIE. SLINGBLADE SEARCH TOOLBAR IN VAIN FOR EMOTICON CAPABLE OF CONVEYING SENSE OF HURT AND FURY PERVADING HIS SOUL AT LOSS OF $8. LAST TIME SLINGBLADE THIS MAD ABOUT $8 IT TURNED OUT STRIPPER HAD COCK AND BALLS. SLINGBLADE GOT OVER THAT ONE AND FORGAVE. SLINGBLADE DON'T THINK HE WILL GET OVER THIS ONE QUITE SO QUICKLY.

Slingblade (the actual movie he's nicknamed after)

This movie is about a funny-talking retard. If that isn't a formula for Hollywood success I don't know what is. I'd pay big $$ to see any of your A-list talent play a retard. Can you image a retarded Pacino delivering his ham-fisted retard dialogue while dressed in a ketchup stained smock: "HOOOOO-ahhhhhh, i just crapped myself. Its allllllllllllllll sticky." I get giddy just thinking about it.

What this movie does is take the retard genre to undreamt-of heights. This is the *Gone With the Wind* of the retard flick. And they did it by turning Billy Bob into some kind of retarded crime-fighting Superman. Genius. I don't throw that term around lightly unless discussing myself. But this is sheer genius.

Billy Bob begins the film with an event that your average retard can relate to. He is released from prison despite the fact that he killed someone. Super. Score one more for the Supreme Court and their goddamn ridiculous ban on executing retards. I swear to God if we don't start executing retards soon I'm going to take care of this problem myself. Anyway, this ex-felon retard continues on the tried and true retard path and befriends a young boy. But this is where it diverges from reality to fantasy. Instead of slaughtering the young boy and eating his gizzard like retards are supposed to do, he decides to protect the boy from his mother's abusive boyfriend. And by protect, I mean kill. Yup, what we have here is a repeat felon. Who would have guessed? Not your pot-smoking hippie public defenders and their communist liberal friends in the judiciary. I think we're supposed to feel bad for the retard. This, of course, wrongly assumes that retards can feel. A fact I disputed highly in my eighth grade science project entitled "Pain Responses of Retards Locked in My Basement and Tortured to Death: A Retrospective."

I should also note that after watching this movie if you go to bars, talk like the retard, and say stuff like "rrmmmmhh, I reckon I want to touch your vaginer" it won't get you laid. Of course, neither will showing off your Star Wars tattoo, so I'm pretty much out of ideas that don't involve GHB.

10 Things I Hate About You

By far my favorite genre of all is the teen romantic comedy. I think it's because these movies speak to something in me. As most of you can probably surmise from my reviews, I am nothing if not a romantic at heart. However, I had the same problem with this movie as I did with all of the other movies like it: the reconciliation of the estranged lovers. This one takes an especially appalling and nauseating twist as the character played by Heath Ledger successfully regains his lost love through the use of a song and dance routine. We all know that in reality the thing normal people do when their girlfriend dumps them is to go out and find a mild-mannered hooker and beat the living shit out of her.

Now I don't know if it was the recurring nightmares this scene gave me or what, but I decided to try this little maneuver on a girl I had offended. Apparently girls grow upset when you are late for a date because you were playing video games and your excuse is: "Captain Tarpals needed my help defending the peace-loving people of Naboo from the invading droid army." Even more so when you tell them they have to remit to you a written apology on behalf of Captain Tarpals for their complicity in disrupting the war effort.

So in an attempt to win her back I spontaneously burst into what I thought was a quite fetching song and dance number performed with my usual panache and ribald flair. Unfortunately she gave me a look of revulsion and pity the likes of which I haven't seen since I told my dad I didn't want to go play football because Star Trek was on. Her loss.

BLACK HAWK DOWN

Loved this movie. Loved it. Foreigners die in droves in this masterpiece. However, I have a little piece of advice concerning the lingo used in the film.

After viewing the film it is NOT a good idea to refer to the North Africans manning the parking garage in your office building as "skinnies." This will result in some office-mandated "sensitivity training." There, some painted whore will listen to your ramblings and tell you that you have "issues with women." Then she will look really surprised when you threaten to "punch her in the goddamn face." The court system calls this "assault." An assault charge makes it hard to find "gainful employment" due to "liability concerns." Instead, you will spend your days watching movies and "plotting your holy vengeance."

BROTHERHOOD OF THE WOLF

There are only two times I have grown physically violent after viewing a movie. The first time was when I saw *The Pledge* in theatres. I can't discuss the specifics of that incident because 1) a red-dimmed tide overtook my vision when I was en route to the projectionist's booth to smite whatever I could find, and 2) the resulting litigation is still pending. The second time is this goddamn piece of crap— *Brotherhood of the Wolf.*

First of all it's a French movie. Frankly the fact that I had Netflix send it to me after discovering this fact means I have only myself to blame. I think the French version of the movie title is *Goddamn Piece of Shit* or something similar; I don't know. I have testosterone in my system, so I can't speak French.

Let me run down the characters in this masterpiece for you. We have an effete taxidermist who happens to be about a fifth-degree black belt. His traveling companion is a mute Indian who is wandering around France in the 1600s and somehow managed to take enough time out of his busy schedule of drinking firewater and ceding his ancestral property to pick up Judo. Their ally is, what else, a papal whore spy. And I'm not just calling her that; she really was a whore. Seriously, I'm not making any of this up. A goddam taxidermist ninja is your hero in this one. Welcome to France, people.

They spend the next what seems like fourteen hours running around fighting a dog I think. To be honest, I can't really remember because I hit myself over the head with a sledgehammer immediately after viewing the film in an attempt to induce amnesia.

Picture the scene immediately after this puppy ends: Hate is frothing at the mouth in a blind fury and begins pacing the apartment and talking to himself, incapable of understanding what the hell just happened. I am frantically searching the basement for the heaviest thing I can find to beat myself unconscious with. Hate begins to slam his hand in the door, as that feeling is one far, far superior to what we felt upon watching the movie. I manage to locate the sledgehammer and put myself down. This event, sadly, represents the most physical damage ever done to an American by a French person.